TECHNICAL ANALYSIS FROM A TO Z

TO

COVERS EVERY TRADING
TOOL ... FROM THE
ABSOLUTE BREADTH INDEX
TO THE ZIG ZAG

STEVEN B. ACHELIS

IRWIN
Professional Publishing®
Chicago • London • Singapore

ISBN 1-55738-816-4

Printed in the United States of America

DO-C

5 6 7 8 9 0

JB

TABLE OF CONTENTS

PREFACE

Over the last decade I have met many of the top technical analysis "gurus" as well as shared experiences with thousands of newcomers. The common element I've discovered among investors who use technical analysis, regardless of their expertise, is the desire to learn more.

No single book, nor any collection of books, can provide a complete explanation of technical analysis. Not only is the field too massive, covering everything from Federal Reserve reports to Fibonacci arcs, but it is also evolving so quickly that anything written today becomes incomplete (but not obsolete) tomorrow.

Armed with the above knowledge and well aware of the myriad technical analysis books that are already available, I feel there is a genuine need for a *concise* book on technical analysis that serves the needs of both the novice and veteran investor. That is what I have strived to create.

The first half of this book is for the newcomer. It is an introduction to technical analysis that presents basic concepts and terminology. The second half is a reference that is designed for anyone using technical analysis. It contains concise explanations of numerous technical analysis tools in a reference format.

When my father began using technical analysis 30 years ago, many people considered technical analysis just another 1960s adventure into the occult. Today, technical analysis is accepted as a viable analytical approach by most universities and brokerage firms. Rarely are large investments made without reviewing the technical climate. Yet even with its acceptance, the number of people who actually perform technical analysis remains relatively small. It is my hope that this book will increase the awareness and use of technical analysis, and in turn, improve the results of those who practice it.

"Information is pretty thin stuff, unless mixed with experience."

—*Clarence Day, 1920*

ACKNOWLEDGMENTS

The truth that no man is an island certainly holds true here. This book would not be possible without the help of thousands of analysts who have studied the markets and shared their results. To those from whom I have compiled this information, thank you.

There are two people who have helped so much that I want to mention them by name: John Slauson, without whose editorial and research assistance this book would not have been published until the next century; and Denise, my wife, who has been an active participant in my work for more than a dozen years.

TERMINOLOGY

For brevity, I use the term "security" when referring to any tradable financial instrument. This includes stocks, bonds, commodities, futures, indices, mutual funds, options, etc. While I may imply a specific investment product (for example, I may say "shares," which implies an equity), these investment concepts will work with any publicly traded financial instrument in which an open market exists.

"Words are like money; there is nothing so useless, unless when in actual use."

—*Samuel Butler, 1902*

Similarly, I intermix the terms "investing" and "trading." Typically, an investor takes a long-term position, while a trader takes a much shorter-term position. In either case, the basic concepts and techniques presented in this book are equally applicable.

TO LEARN MORE

Investors share a common desire—they want to learn more. If you'd like to receive a list of additional learning material (technical analysis books, software, and videos), please call my office at 800-882-3034.

Steve Achelis

PART
ONE

INTRODUCTION TO TECHNICAL ANALYSIS

Part One was written for investors who are new to technical analysis. It presents the basic concepts and terminology in a concise manner. If you are familiar with technical analysis, you will probably find Part Two the appropriate starting point.

TECHNICAL ANALYSIS

Should I buy today? What will prices be tomorrow, next week, or next year? Wouldn't investing be easy if we knew the answers to these seemingly simple questions? Alas, if you are reading this book in the hope that technical analysis has the answers to these questions, I'm afraid I have to disappoint you early—it doesn't. However, if you are reading this book with the hope that technical analysis will improve your investing, I have good news—it will!

SOME HISTORY

The term "technical analysis" is a complicated-sounding name for a very basic approach to investing. Simply put, technical analysis is the study of prices, with charts being the primary tool, to make better investments.

The roots of modern-day technical analysis stem from the Dow Theory, developed around 1900 by Charles Dow. Stemming either directly or indirectly from the Dow Theory, these roots include such principles as the trending nature of prices, prices discounting all known information, confirmation and divergence, volume mirroring changes in price, and support/resistance. And of course, the widely followed Dow Jones Industrial Average is a direct offspring of the Dow Theory.

Charles Dow's contribution to modern-day technical analysis cannot be understated. His focus on the basics of security price movement gave rise to a completely new method of analyzing the markets.

THE HUMAN ELEMENT

The price of a security represents a consensus. It is the price at which one person agrees to buy and another agrees to sell. The price at which an investor is willing to buy or sell depends primarily on his expectations. If he expects the security's price to rise, he will buy it; if the investor expects the price to fall, he will sell it. These simple statements are the cause of a major challenge in forecasting security prices, because they refer to *human* expectations. As we all know firsthand, humans are not easily quantifiable nor predictable. This fact alone will keep any mechanical trading system from working consistently.

Because humans are involved, I am sure that many of the world's investment decisions are based on irrelevant criteria. Our relationships with our family, our neighbors, our employer, the traffic, our income, and our previous successes and failures all influence our confidence, expectations, and decisions.

Security prices are determined by money managers and home managers, students and strikers, doctors and dog catchers, lawyers and landscapers, and the wealthy and the wanting. This breadth of market participants guarantees an element of unpredictability and excitement.

FUNDAMENTAL ANALYSIS

If we were all totally logical and could separate our emotions from our investment decisions, then fundamental analysis, the determination of price based on future earnings (see page 144), would work magnificently. And since we would all have the same completely logical expectations, prices would change only when quarterly reports or relevant news was released. Investors would seek "overlooked" fundamental data in an effort to find undervalued securities.

The hotly debated "efficient market theory" (see page 124) states that security prices represent everything that is known about the security at a given moment. This theory concludes that it is impossible to forecast prices, since prices already reflect everything that is currently known about the security.

THE FUTURE CAN BE FOUND IN THE PAST

If prices are based on investor expectations, then knowing what a security *should* sell for (i.e., fundamental analysis) becomes less important than knowing what other investors expect it to sell for. That's not to say that knowing what a security should sell for isn't important—it is. But there is usually a fairly strong consensus of a stock's future earnings that the average investor cannot disprove.

"I believe the future is only the past again, entered through another gate."

—Sir Arthur Wing Pinero, 1893

Technical analysis is the process of analyzing a security's historical prices in an effort to determine probable future prices. This is done by comparing current price action (i.e., current expectations) with comparable historical price action to predict a reasonable outcome. The devout technician might define this process as the fact that history repeats itself, while others would suffice to say that we should learn from the past.

THE ROULETTE WHEEL

In my experience, only a "tiny" minority of technicians can determine future prices consistently and accurately. However, even if you are unable to forecast prices accurately, technical analysis can be used to consistently reduce your risks and improve your profits.

The best analogy I can find on how technical analysis can improve your investing is a roulette wheel. I use this analogy with reservation, as gamblers have very little control when compared to investors (although considering the actions of many investors, gambling may be a *very* appropriate analogy).

"There are two times in a man's life when he should not speculate: when he can't afford it, and when he can."

—Mark Twain, 1897

A casino makes money on a roulette wheel, not by knowing what number will come up next, but by *slightly* improving their odds with the addition of a 0 and 00.

Similarly, when an investor purchases a security, she doesn't *know* that its price will rise. But if she buys a stock when it is in a rising trend, after a minor sell-off, and when interest rates are falling, she will have improved her odds of making a profit. That's not gambling—it's intelligence. Yet many investors buy securities without attempting to control the odds.

Contrary to popular belief, you do not need to know what a security's price will be in the future to make money. Your goal should simply be to improve the odds of making profitable trades. Even if your analysis is as simple as determining the long-, intermediate-, and short-term trends of the security, you will have gained an edge that you would not have without technical analysis.

Consider the chart of Merck in Figure 1, where the trend is obviously down and there is no sign of a reversal. While the company may have great earnings prospects and fundamentals, it just doesn't make sense to buy the security until there is some technical evidence in the price that this trend is changing.

FIGURE I

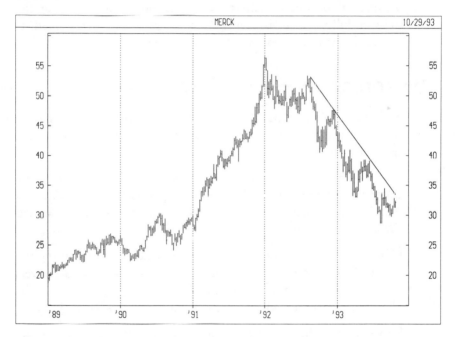

AUTOMATED TRADING

If we accept the fact that human emotions and expectations play a role in security pricing, we should also admit that our emotions play a role in our decision making. Many investors try to remove their emotions from their investing by using computers to make decisions for them. The concept of a "HAL," the intelligent computer in the movie *2001,* is appealing.

Mechanical trading systems can help us remove our emotions from our decisions. Computer testing is also useful to determine what has happened historically under various conditions and to help us optimize our trading techniques. Yet since we are analyzing a less than logical subject (human emotions and expectations), we must be careful that our mechanical systems don't mislead us into thinking that we are analyzing a logical entity.

That is not to say that computers aren't wonderful technical analysis tools—they are indispensable. In my *totally biased* opinion, technical analysis software has done more to level the playing field for the average investor than any other nonregulatory event. But as a provider of technical analysis tools, I caution you not to let the software lull you into believing markets are as logical and predictable as the computer you use to analyze them.

PRICE FIELDS

Technical analysis is based almost entirely on the analysis of price and volume. The fields that define a security's price and volume are explained below.

Open—This is the price of the first trade for the period (e.g., the first trade of the day). When analyzing daily data, the Open is especially important as it is the consensus price after all interested parties were able to "sleep on it."

High—This is the highest price that the security traded during the period. It is the point at which there were more sellers than buyers (i.e., there are always sellers willing to sell at higher prices, but the High represents the highest price that buyers were willing to pay).

Low—This is the lowest price that the security traded during the period. It is the point at which there were more buyers than sellers (i.e., there are always buyers willing to buy at lower prices, but the Low represents the lowest price sellers were willing to accept).

Close—This is the last price that the security traded during the period. Due to its availability, the Close is the most often used price for analysis. The relationship between the Open (the first price) and the Close (the last price) is considered significant by most technicians. This relationship is emphasized in candlestick charts (see page 79).

Volume—This is the number of shares (or contracts) that were traded during the period. The relationship between prices and volume (e.g., increasing prices accompanied by increasing volume) is important.

Open Interest—This is the total number of outstanding contracts (i.e., those that have not been exercised, closed, or expired) of a future or option. Open interest is often used as an indicator (see page 210).

Bid—This is the price a market maker is willing to pay for a security (i.e., the price you will receive if you sell).

Ask—This is the price a market maker is willing to accept (i.e., the price you will pay to buy the security).

These simple fields are used to create literally hundreds of technical tools that study price relationships, trends, patterns, etc.

Not all of these price fields are available for all security types, and many quote providers publish only a subset of these. Table 1 shows the typical fields that are reported for several security types.

TABLE 1

	FUTURES	MUTUAL FUNDS	STOCKS	OPTIONS
Open	Yes	No	Often	Yes
High	Yes	Closed end	Yes	Yes
Low	Yes	Closed end	Yes	Yes
Close	Yes	Yes (*NAV)	Yes	Yes
Volume	Yes	Closed end	Yes	Yes
Open Int.	Yes	N/A	N/A	Often
Bid	Intraday	Closed end	Intraday	Intraday
Ask	Intraday	Closed end	Intraday	Intraday

*Net Asset Value.

CHARTS

The foundation of technical analysis is the chart. In this case, a picture *is* truly worth a thousand words.

LINE CHARTS

A line chart is the simplest type of chart. As shown in the chart of General Motors in Figure 2, the single line represents the security's closing price on each day. Dates are displayed along the bottom of the chart and prices are displayed on the side(s).

FIGURE 2

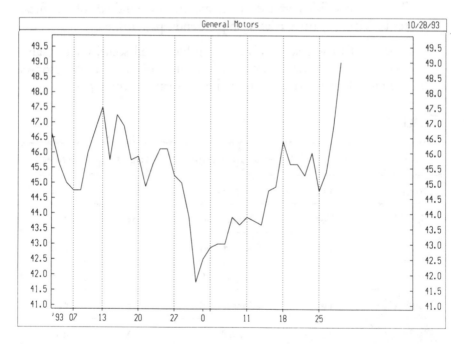

A line chart's strength comes from its simplicity. It provides an uncluttered, easy-to-understand view of a security's price. Line charts are typically displayed using a security's closing prices.

BAR CHARTS

A bar chart displays a security's open (if available), high, low, and closing prices. Bar charts are the most popular type of security chart.

As illustrated in the bar chart in Figure 3, the top of each vertical bar represents the highest price that the security traded during the period, and the bottom of the bar represents the lowest price that it traded. A closing "tick" is displayed on the right side of the bar to designate the last price that the security traded. If opening prices are available, they are signified by a tick on the left side of the bar.

FIGURE 3

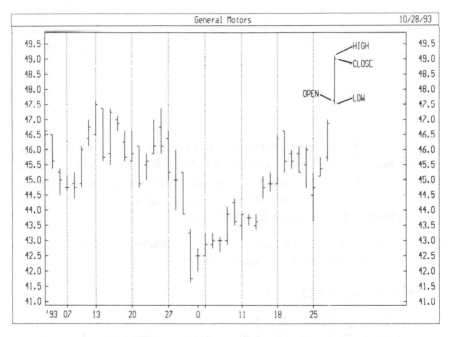

VOLUME BAR CHART

Volume is usually displayed as a bar graph at the bottom of the chart (see Figure 4). Most analysts monitor only the relative level of volume and as such, a volume scale is often not displayed.

Figure 4 displays "zero-based" volume. This means the bottom of each volume bar represents the value of zero. However, most ana-

FIGURE 4

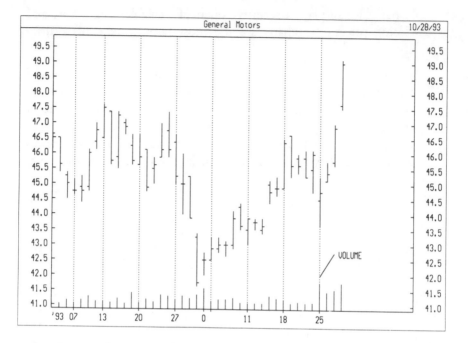

lysts prefer to see volume that is "relative-adjusted" rather than zero-based. This is done by subtracting the lowest volume that occurred during the period displayed from all of the volume bars. Relative-adjusted volume bars make it easier to see trends in volume by ignoring the minimum daily volume.

Figure 5 displays the same volume information as in the previous chart, but this volume is relative-adjusted.

OTHER CHART TYPES

Security prices can also be displayed using other types of charts, such as candlestick, Equivolume, point and figure, etc. For brevity's sake, explanations of these charting methods appear only in Part II.

SUPPORT AND RESISTANCE

Think of security prices as the result of a head-to-head battle between a bull (the buyer) and a bear (the seller). The bulls push

FIGURE 5

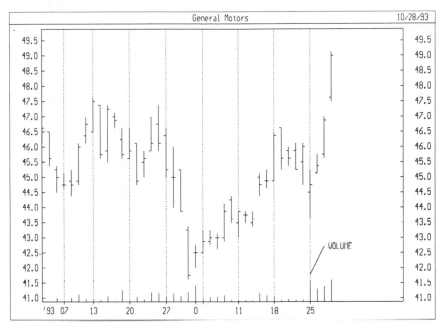

prices higher and the bears push prices lower. The direction prices actually move reveals who is winning the battle.

Using this analogy, consider the price action of Phillip Morris in Figure 6. During the period shown, note how each time prices fell to the $45.50 level, the bulls (i.e., the buyers) took control and prevented prices from falling further. That means that at the price of $45.50, buyers felt that investing in Phillip Morris was worthwhile (and sellers were not willing to sell for less than $45.50). This type of price action is referred to as support, because buyers are supporting the price of $45.50.

Similar to support, a "resistance" level is the point at which sellers take control of prices and prevent them from rising higher. Consider Figure 7. Note how each time prices neared the level of $51.50, sellers outnumbered buyers and prevented the price from rising.

The price at which a trade takes place is the price at which a bull and bear agree to do business. It represents the consensus of their

FIGURE 6

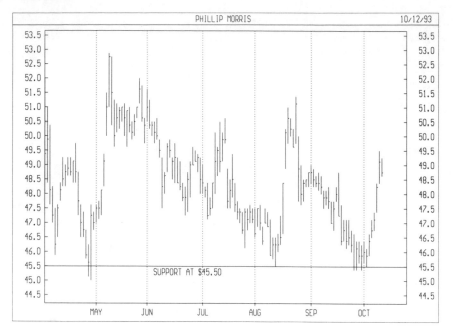

FIGURE 7

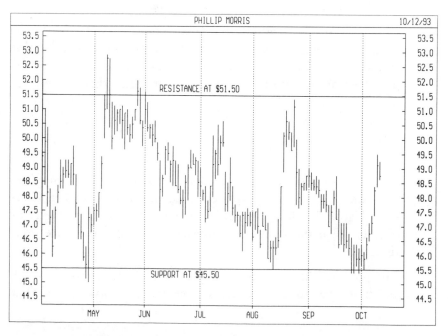

expectations. The bulls think prices will move higher and the bears think prices will move lower.

Support levels indicate the price where the majority of investors believe that prices will move higher, and resistance levels indicate the price at which a majority of investors feel prices will move lower.

But investor *expectations change with time!* For a long time, investors did not expect the Dow Industrials to rise above 1,000 (as shown by the heavy resistance at 1,000 in Figure 8). Yet only a few years later, investors were willing to trade with the Dow near 2,500.

FIGURE 8

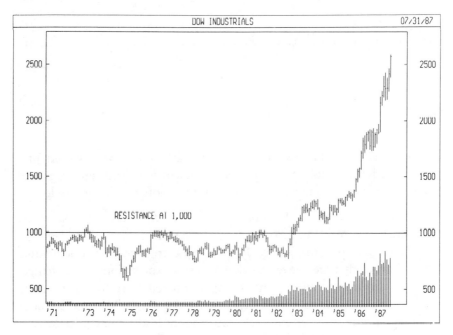

When investor expectations change, they often do so abruptly. Note how when prices rose above the resistance level of Hasbro Inc. in Figure 9, they did so decisively. Note too, that the breakout above the resistance level was accompanied with a significant increase in volume.

Once investors accepted that Hasbro could trade above $20.00, more investors were willing to buy it at higher levels (causing both

FIGURE 9

prices and volume to increase). Similarly, sellers who would previously have sold when prices approached $20.00 also began to
expect prices to move higher and were no longer willing to sell.

The development of support and resistance levels is probably the
most noticeable and recurring event on price charts. The penetration of support/resistance levels can be triggered by fundamental
changes that are above or below investor expectations (e.g., changes
in earnings, management, competition, etc.) or by self-fulfilling
prophecy (investors buy as they see prices rise). The cause is not as
significant as the effect—new expectations lead to new price levels.

Figure 10 shows a breakout caused by fundamental factors. The
breakout occurred when Snapple released a higher than expected
earnings report. How do we know it was higher-than-expectations?
By the resulting change in prices following the report!

Other support/resistance levels are more emotional. For example,
the DJIA had a tough time changing investor expectations when it
neared 3,000 (see Figure 11).

FIGURE 10

SNAPPLE — 06/01/93

BREAKOUT ON
EARNINGS REPORT

FIGURE 11

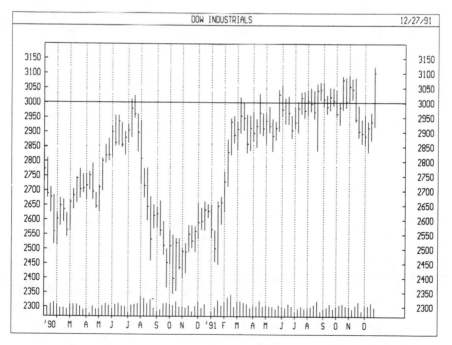

DOW INDUSTRIALS — 12/27/91

SUPPLY AND DEMAND

There is nothing mysterious about support and resistance—it is classic supply and demand. Remembering Econ 101 class, supply/demand lines show what the supply and demand will be at a given price.

The "supply" line shows the quantity (i.e., the number of shares) that sellers are willing to supply at a given price. When prices increase, the quantity of sellers also increases as more investors are willing to sell at these higher prices.

The "demand" line shows the number of shares that buyers are willing to buy at a given price. When prices increase, the quantity of buyers decreases as fewer investors are willing to buy at higher prices.

At any given price, a supply/demand chart (see Figure 12) shows how many buyers and sellers there are. For example, the following chart shows that, at the price of 42 1/2, there will be 10 buyers and 25 sellers.

FIGURE 12

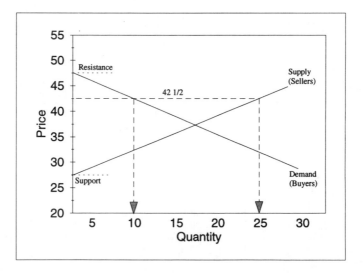

Support occurs at the price where the supply line touches the left side of the chart (e.g., 27 1/2 on the above chart). Prices can't fall below this amount because no sellers are willing to sell at these prices. Resistance occurs at the price where the demand line touches the left side of the chart (e.g., 47 1/2). Prices can't rise above this amount because there are no buyers willing to buy at these prices.

In a free market, these lines are continually changing. As investor expectations change, so do the prices buyers and sellers feel are acceptable. A breakout above a resistance level is evidence of an upward shift in the demand line as more buyers become willing to buy at higher prices. Similarly, the failure of a support level shows that the supply line has shifted downward.

The foundation of most technical analysis tools is rooted in the concept of supply and demand. Charts of security prices give us a superb view of these forces in action.

TRADERS' REMORSE

Following the penetration of a support/resistance level, it is common for traders to question the new price levels. For example, after a breakout above a resistance level, buyers and sellers may both question the validity of the new price and may decide to sell. This creates a phenomenon I refer to as "traders' remorse," when prices return to a support/resistance level following a price breakout.

Consider the breakout of Phillip Morris in Figure 13. Note how the breakout was followed by a correction in the price, where prices returned to the resistance level.

The price action following this remorseful period is crucial. One of two things can happen. Either the consensus of expectations will be that the new price is not warranted, in which case prices will move back to their previous level; or investors will accept the new price, in which case prices will continue to move in the direction of the penetration.

If, following traders' remorse, the consensus of expectations is that a new higher price is not warranted, a classic "bull trap" (or "false breakout") is created. As shown in Figure 14, prices penetrated the resistance level at $67.50 (luring in a herd of bulls who expected

FIGURE 13

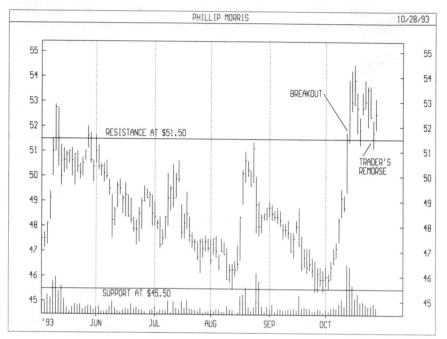

FIGURE 14

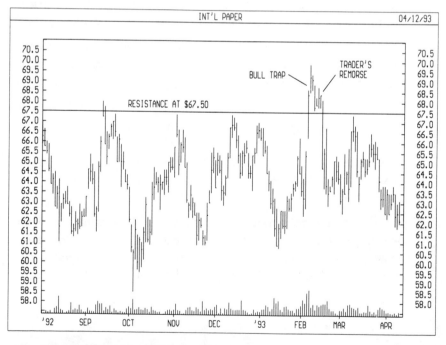

prices to move higher), and then prices dropped back to below the resistance level, leaving the bulls holding overpriced stock.

Similar sentiment creates a bear trap. Prices drop below a support level long enough to get the bears to sell (or sell short) and then bounce back above the support level, leaving the bears out of the market (see Figure 15).

FIGURE 15

The other thing that can happen following traders' remorse is that investors' expectations may change, causing the new price to be accepted. In this case, prices will continue to move in the direction of the penetration (i.e., up if a resistance level was penetrated or down if a support level was penetrated). [See Figure 16.]

A good way to quantify expectations following a breakout is with the volume associated with the price breakout. If prices break through the support/resistance level with a large increase in volume and the traders' remorse period is on relatively low volume, it implies that the new expectations will rule (a minority of investors are remorseful). Conversely, if the breakout is on moderate volume and

FIGURE 16

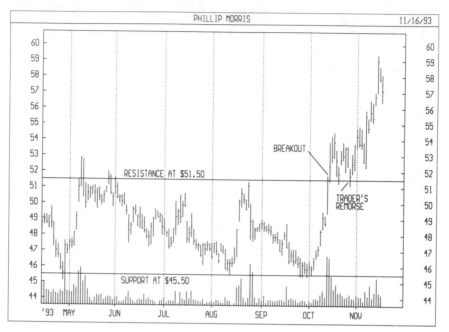

the "remorseful" period is on increased volume, it implies that very few investor expectations have changed and a return to the original expectations (i.e., original prices) is warranted.

RESISTANCE BECOMES SUPPORT

When a resistance level is successfully penetrated, that level becomes a support level. Similarly, when a support level is successfully penetrated, that level becomes a resistance level.

An example of resistance changing to support is shown in Figure 17. When prices broke above the resistance level of $45.00, the level of $45.00 became the new support level.

This is because a new "generation" of bulls who didn't buy when prices were less than $45.00 (they didn't have bullish expectations then) are now anxious to buy any time prices return near the $45.00 level.

Similarly, when prices drop below a support level, that level often becomes a resistance level that prices have a difficult time penetrat-

FIGURE 17

ing. When prices approach the previous support level, investors seek to limit their losses by selling (see Figure 18).

REVIEW

I kept discussions of price action, investor expectations, and support/resistance as concise as possible. However, from my experience working with investors, I am thoroughly convinced that most investors could significantly improve their performance if they would pay more attention to the underlying causes affecting security prices: investor expectations and supply/demand.

The following is a very brief review of the support/resistance concepts discussed in this section.

1. A security's price represents the fair market value as agreed between buyers (bulls) and sellers (bears).

2. Changes in price are the result of changes in investor expectations of the security's future price.

FIGURE 18

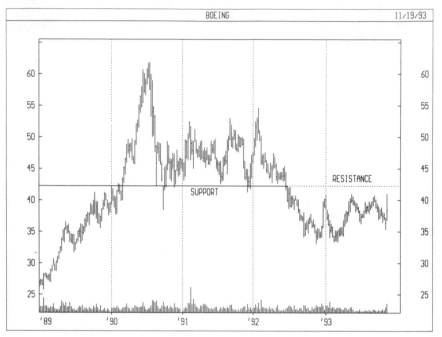

3. Support levels occur when the consensus is that the price will not move lower.

4. Resistance levels occur when the consensus is that the price will not move higher.

5. The penetration of a support or resistance level indicates a change in investor expectations and a shift in the supply/demand lines.

6. Volume is useful in determining how strong the change of expectations really is.

7. Traders' remorse often follows the penetration of a support or resistance level as prices retreat to the penetrated level.

8. Once penetrated, support levels often provide price resistance and vice versa.

TRENDS

In the preceding section, we saw how support and resistance levels can be penetrated by a change in investor expectations (which results in shifts of the supply/demand lines). This type of change is often abrupt and "news-based."

In this section, we'll review "trends." A trend represents a consistent change in prices (i.e., a change in investor expectations). Trends differ from support/resistance levels in that trends represent change, whereas support/resistance levels represent barriers to change.

As shown in Figure 19, a rising trend is defined by successively higher low-prices. A rising trend can be thought of as a rising support level—the bulls are in control and are pushing prices higher.

FIGURE 19

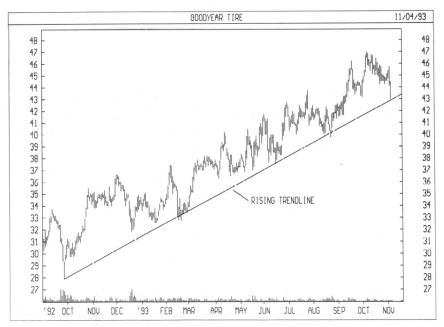

Figure 20 shows a falling trend. A falling trend is defined by successively lower high-prices. A falling trend can be thought of as a falling resistance level—the bears are in control and are pushing prices lower.

FIGURE 20

Just as prices penetrate support and resistance levels when expectations change, prices can penetrate rising and falling trendlines. Figure 21 shows the penetration of Merck's falling trendline as investors no longer expected lower prices.

Note in Figure 21 how volume increased when the trendline was penetrated. This is an important confirmation that the previous trend is no longer intact.

As with support and resistance levels, it is common to have traders' remorse following the penetration of a trendline. This is illustrated in Figure 22.

Again, volume is the key to determining the significance of the penetration of a trend. In the above example, volume increased when the trend was penetrated, and was weak as the bulls tried to move prices back above the trendline.

FIGURE 21

MERCK — 11/19/93

BREAKOUT

INCREASED VOLUME

'92 SEP OCT NOV DEC '93 FEB MAR APR MAY JUN JUL AUG SEP OCT NOV

FIGURE 22

GOODYEAR — 10/09/92

TRADER'S REMORSE

DECREASED VOLUME

'91 J J A S O N D '92 F M A M J J A S O

MOVING AVERAGES

The moving average is one of the oldest and most popular technical analysis tools. This section describes the basic calculation and interpretation of moving averages. Full details on moving averages are provided in Part II (see page 184).

A moving average is the *average price of a security at a given time.* When calculating a moving average, you specify the time span to calculate the average price (e.g., 25 days).

A "simple" moving average is calculated by adding the security's prices for the most recent "n" time periods and then dividing by "n." For example, add the closing prices of a security for the most recent 25 days and then divide by 25. The result is the security's average price over the last 25 days. This calculation is done for each period in the chart.

Note that a moving average cannot be calculated until you have "n" time periods of data. For example, you cannot display a 25-day moving average until the 25th day in a chart.

Figure 23 shows a 25-day simple moving average of the closing price of Caterpillar.

Since the moving average in this chart is the average price of the security over the last 25 days, it represents the consensus of investor expectations over the last 25 days. If the security's price is above its moving average, it means that investors' current expectations (i.e., the current price) are higher than their average expectations over the last 25 days, and that investors are becoming increasingly bullish on the security. Conversely, if today's price is below its moving average, it shows that current expectations are below the average expectations over the last 25 days.

The classic interpretation of a moving average is to use it to observe changes in prices. Investors typically buy when a security's price rises above its moving average and sell when the price falls below its moving average.

FIGURE 23

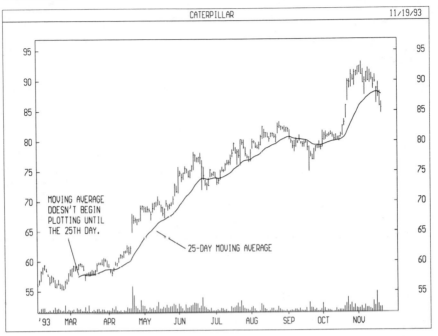

CATERPILLAR   11/19/93

MOVING AVERAGE DOESN'T BEGIN PLOTTING UNTIL THE 25TH DAY.

25-DAY MOVING AVERAGE

'93   MAR   APR   MAY   JUN   JUL   AUG   SEP   OCT   NOV

TIME PERIODS IN MOVING AVERAGES

"Buy" arrows were drawn on the chart in Figure 24 to show when Aflac's price rose above its 200-day moving average; "sell" arrows were drawn when Aflac's price fell below its 200-day moving average. (To simplify the chart, the brief periods when Aflac crossed its moving average for only a few days were not labeled.)

Long-term trends are often isolated using a 200-day moving average. You can also use computer software to automatically determine the optimum number of time periods. Ignoring commissions, higher profits are usually found using shorter moving averages.

MERITS

The merit of this type of moving average system (i.e., buying and selling when prices penetrate their moving average) is that you will always be on the "right" side of the market—prices cannot rise very much without the price rising above its average price. The disadvantage is that you will always buy and sell late. If the trend doesn't

FIGURE 24

last for a significant period of time, typically twice the length of the moving average, you'll lose money. This is illustrated in Figure 25.

TRADERS' REMORSE

Moving averages often demonstrate traders' remorse (see page 17). As shown in Figure 26, it is very common for a security to penetrate its long-term moving average and then return to its average before continuing on its way.

You can also use moving averages to smooth erratic data. The charts in Figure 27 show the 13-year history of the number of stocks making new highs (upper chart) and a 10-week moving average of this value (lower chart). Note how the moving average makes it easier to view the true trend of the data.

FIGURE 25

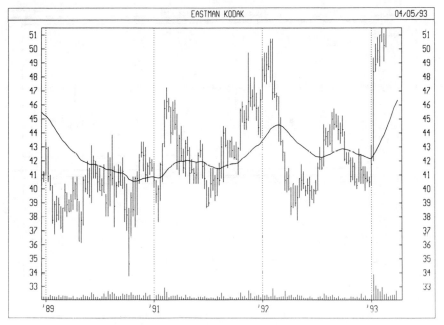

FIGURE 26

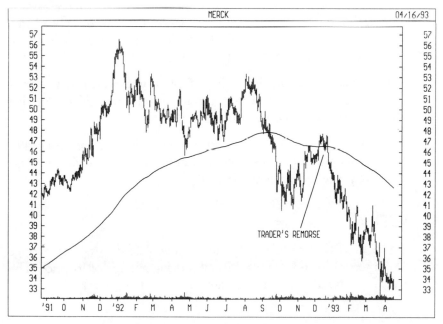

FIGURE 27

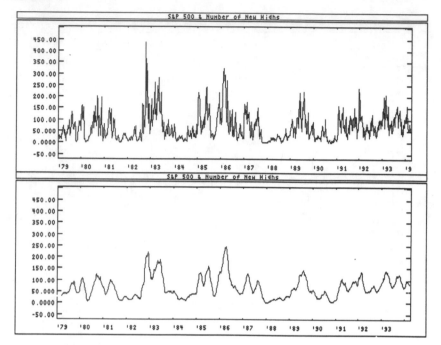

INDICATORS

An indicator is a mathematical calculation that can be applied to a security's price and/or volume fields. The result is a value that is used to anticipate future changes in prices.

A moving average fits this definition of an indicator: it is a calculation that can be performed on a security's price to yield a value that can be used to anticipate future changes in prices.

Part II contains numerous examples of indicators (see page 49). Let's briefly review one simple indicator here, the Moving Average Convergence Divergence (MACD).

MACD

The MACD is calculated by subtracting a 26-day moving average of a security's price from a 12-day moving average of its price. The result is an indicator that oscillates above and below zero.

When the MACD is above zero, it means the 12-day moving average is higher than the 26-day moving average. This is bullish, since it shows that current expectations (i.e., the 12-day moving average) are more bullish than previous expectations (i.e., the 26-day average). This implies a bullish, or upward, shift in the supply/demand lines. When the MACD falls below zero, it means that the 12-day moving average is below the 26-day moving average, implying a bearish shift in the supply/demand lines.

Figure 28 shows Autozone and its MACD. The chart is labeled "Bullish" when the MACD was above zero and "Bearish" when it was below zero. The 12- and 26-day moving averages are also displayed on the price chart.

FIGURE 28

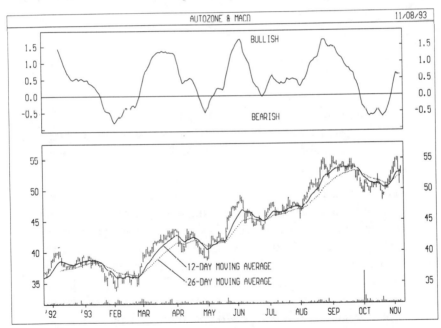

A 9-day moving average *of the MACD* (not of the security's price) is usually plotted on top of the MACD indicator. This line is referred to as the "signal" line. The signal line anticipates the convergence of the two moving averages (i.e., the movement of the MACD toward the zero line).

FIGURE 29

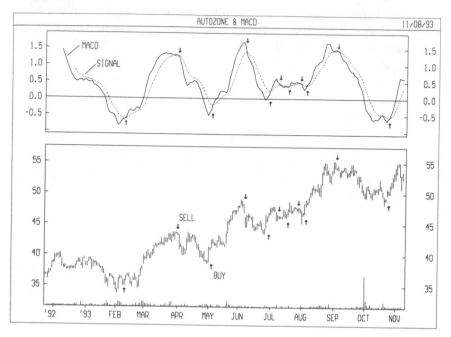

The chart in Figure 29 shows the MACD (the solid line) and its signal line (the dotted line). "Buy" arrows were drawn when the MACD rose above its signal line; "sell" arrows were drawn when the MACD fell below its signal line.

Let's consider the rationale behind this technique. The MACD is the difference between two moving averages of price. When the shorter-term moving average rises above the longer-term moving average (i.e., the MACD rises above zero), it means that investor expectations are becoming more bullish (i.e., there has been an upward shift in the supply/demand lines). By plotting a 9-day moving average of the MACD, we can see the changing of expectations (i.e., the shifting of the supply/demand lines) as they occur.

LEADING VERSUS LAGGING INDICATORS

Moving averages and the MACD are examples of trend-following, or "lagging," indicators. [See Figure 30.] These indicators are superb when prices move in relatively long trends. They don't warn

FIGURE 30

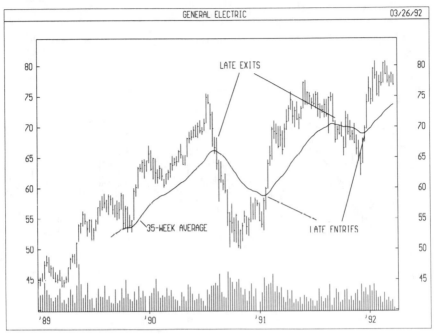

GENERAL ELECTRIC 03/26/92

LATE EXITS

35-WEEK AVERAGE

LATE ENTRIES

'89 '90 '91 '92

you of upcoming changes in prices; they simply tell you what prices are doing (i.e., rising or falling) so that you can invest accordingly. Trend-following indicators have you buy and sell late and, in exchange for missing the early opportunities, they greatly reduce your risk by keeping you on the right side of the market.

As shown in Figure 31, trend-following indicators do not work well in sideways markets.

Another class of indicators is "leading" indicators. These indicators help you profit by predicting what prices will do next. Leading indicators provide greater rewards at the expense of increased risk. They perform best in sideways, "trading" markets.

Leading indicators typically work by measuring how "overbought" or "oversold" a security is. This is done with the assumption that a security that is "oversold" will bounce back. [See Figure 32.]

What type of indicators you use, leading or lagging, is a matter of personal preference. It has been my experience that most investors (including me) are better at following trends than predicting them.

FIGURE 31

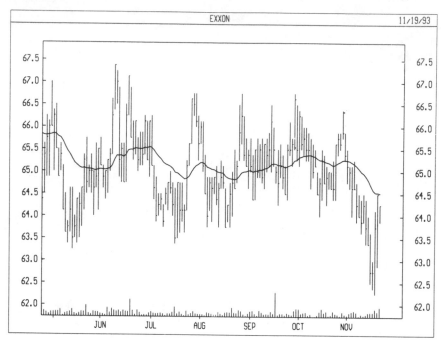

FIGURE 32

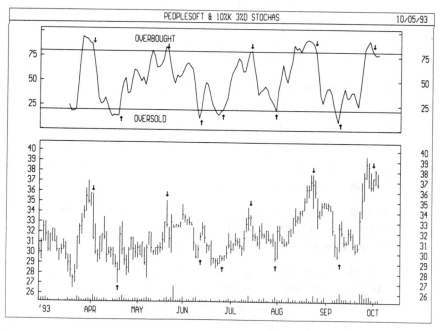

Thus, I personally prefer trend-following indicators. However, I have met many successful investors who prefer leading indicators.

TRENDING PRICES VERSUS TRADING PRICES

There have been several trading systems and indicators developed that determine if prices are trending or trading. The approach is that you should use lagging indicators during trending markets and leading indicators during trading markets. While it is relatively easy to determine if prices are trending or trading, it is extremely difficult to know if prices *will* trend or trade in the future. [See Figure 33.]

FIGURE 33

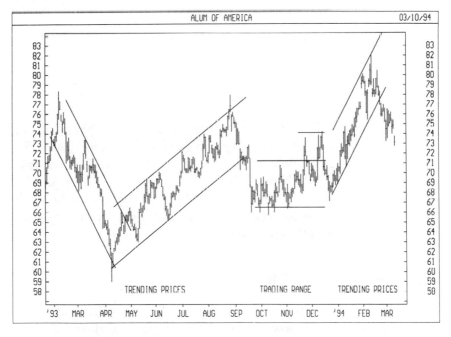

DIVERGENCES

A divergence occurs when the trend of a security's price doesn't agree with the trend of an indicator. Many of the examples in Part II demonstrate divergences.

FIGURE 34

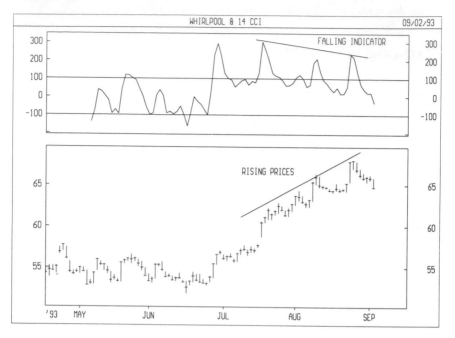

The chart in Figure 34 shows a divergence between Whirlpool and its 14-day CCI (Commodity Channel Index). [See page 95.] Whirlpool's prices were making new highs while the CCI was failing to make new highs. When divergences occur, prices usually change direction to confirm the trend of the indicator, as shown in Figure 34. This occurs because indicators are better at gauging price trends than the prices themselves.

MARKET INDICATORS

All of the technical analysis tools discussed up to this point were calculated using a security's price (e.g., high, low, close, volume). There is another group of technical analysis tools designed to help you gauge changes in *all* securities within a specific market. These indicators are usually referred to as "market indicators," because they gauge an entire market, not just an individual security. Market indicators typically analyze the stock market, although they can be used for other markets (e.g., futures).

While the data items available for an individual security are limited to its open, high, low, close, volume (see page 6), and sparse financial reports, there are numerous data items available for the overall stock market. For example, the number of stocks that made new highs for the day, the number of stocks that increased in price, the volume associated with the stocks that increased in price, etc. Market indicators cannot be calculated for an individual security because the required data is not available.

Market indicators add significant depth to technical analysis because they contain much more information than price and volume. A typical approach is to use market indicators to determine where the overall market is headed and then use price/volume indicators to determine when to buy or sell an individual security. The analogy being "all boats rise in a rising tide," it is therefore much less risky to own stocks when the stock market is rising.

CATEGORIES OF MARKET INDICATORS

Market indicators typically fall into three categories: monetary, sentiment, and momentum.

Monetary indicators concentrate on economic data such as interest rates. They help you determine the economic environment in which businesses operate. These external forces directly affect a business' profitability and share price.

Examples of monetary indicators are interest rates, the money supply, consumer and corporate debt, and inflation. Due to the vast quantity of monetary indicators, only a few of the basic monetary indicators are discussed in this book.

Sentiment indicators focus on investor expectations—often before those expectations are discernible in prices. With an individual security, the price is often the only measure of investor sentiment available. However, for a large market such as the New York Stock Exchange, many more sentiment indicators are available. These include the number of odd lot sales (i.e., what are the smallest investors doing?), the put/call ratio (i.e., how many people are buying puts versus calls?), the premium on stock index futures, the ratio of bullish versus bearish investment advisors, etc.

"Contrarian" investors use sentiment indicators to determine what the majority of investors expect prices to do; they then do the opposite, the rationale being that if everybody agrees that prices will rise, then there probably aren't enough investors left to push prices much higher. This concept is well proven—almost everyone is bullish at market tops (when they should be selling) and bearish at market bottoms (when they should be buying).

The third category of market indicators, momentum, shows what prices are actually doing, but do so by looking deeper than price. Examples of momentum indicators include all of the price/volume indicators applied to the various market indices (e.g., the MACD of the Dow Industrials), the number of stocks that made new highs versus the number of stocks making new lows, the relationship between the number of stocks that advanced in price versus the number that declined, the comparison of the volume associated with increased price with the volume associated with decreased price, etc.

Given the above three groups of market indicators, we have insight into:

1. The external monetary conditions affecting security prices. This tells us what security prices should do.

2. The sentiment of various sectors of the investment community. This tells us what investors expect prices to do.

3. The current momentum of the market. This tells us what prices are actually doing.

Figure 35 shows the prime rate along with a 50-week moving average. "Buy" arrows were drawn when the prime rate crossed below its moving average (interest rates were falling), and "sell" arrows were drawn when the prime rate crossed above its moving average (interest rates were rising). This chart illustrates the intense relationship between stock prices and interest rates.

Figure 36 shows a 10-day moving average of the put/call ratio (a sentiment indicator). The chart is labeled with "buy" arrows to show each time the moving average rose above 85.0. This is the level where investors were extremely bearish and expected prices to decline. You can see that each time investors became extremely bearish, prices actually rose.

FIGURE 35

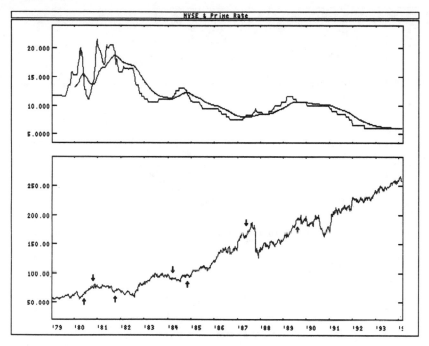

FIGURE 36

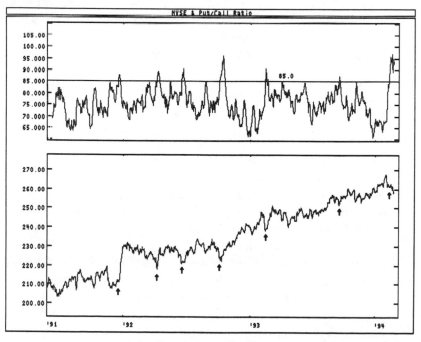

FIGURE 37

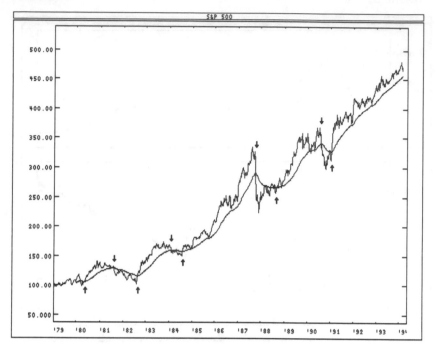

Figure 37 shows a 50-week moving average (a momentum indicator) of the S&P 500. "Buy" arrows were drawn when the S&P rose above its 50-week moving average; "sell" arrows were drawn when the S&P fell below its moving average. You can see how this momentum indicator caught every major market move.

Figure 38 merges the preceding monetary and momentum charts. The chart is labeled "Bullish" when the prime rate was below its 50-week moving average (meaning that interest rates were falling) and when the S&P was above its 50-week moving average.

The chart in Figure 38 is a good example of the roulette metaphor presented on page 4. You don't need to know exactly where prices will be in the future—you simply need to improve your odds. At any given time during the period shown in this chart, I couldn't have told you where the market would be six months later. However, by knowing that the odds favor a rise in stock prices when interest rates are falling and when the S&P is above its 50-week moving average, and by limiting long positions (i.e., buying) to periods when both of these indicators are bullish, you could dra-

FIGURE 38

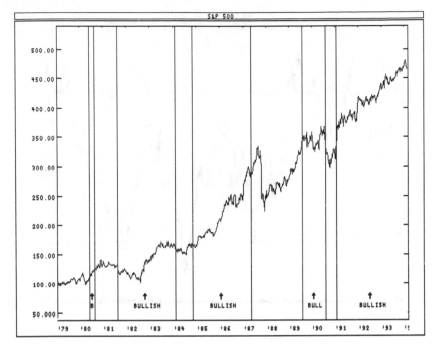

matically reduce your risks and increase your chances of making a profit.

LINE STUDIES

Line studies are technical analysis tools that consist of lines drawn on top of a security's price and/or indicator. These include the support, resistance, and trendline concepts already discussed.

Figure 39 illustrates several line studies. These and numerous additional studies are explained in Part II.

PERIODICITY

Regardless of the "periodicity" of the data in your charts (i.e., hourly, daily, weekly, monthly, etc.), the basic principles of technical analysis endure. Consider the charts of a Swiss franc contract shown in Figures 40, 41, and 42.

FIGURE 39

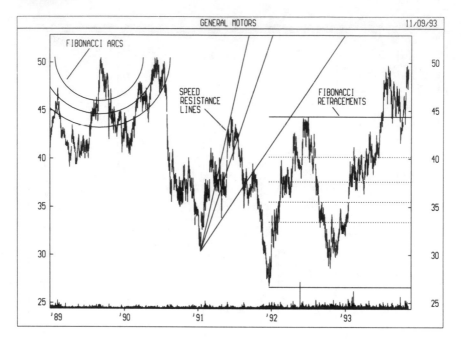

FIGURE 40

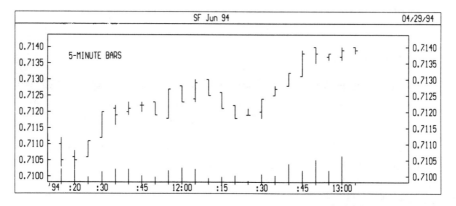

FIGURE 41

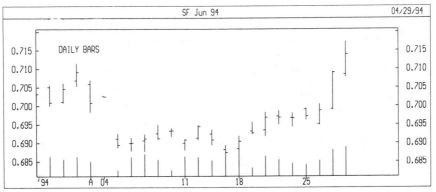

FIGURE 42

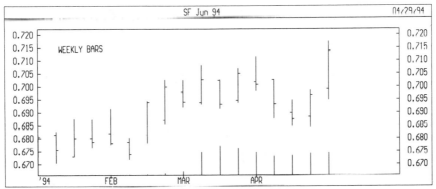

Typically, the shorter the periodicity, the more difficult it is to predict and profit from changes in prices. The difficulty associated with shorter periodicities is compounded by the fact that you have less time to make your decisions.

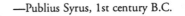

"While we stop and think, we often miss our opportunity."

—Publius Syrus, 1st century B.C.

Opportunities exist in any time frame. But I have rarely met a successful short-term trader who wasn't also a successful long-term investor. And I have met many investors who get caught by the grass-is-greener syndrome, believing that using shorter and shorter time periods is the secret to making money—it isn't.

THE TIME ELEMENT

The discussion that began on page 6 explained the open, high, low, and closing *price* fields. This section presents the *time* element.

Much of technical analysis focuses on changes in prices over time. Consider the effect of time in the following charts, each of which show a security's price increase from $25.00 to around $45.00.

Figure 43 shows that Merck's price increased consistently over a 12-month time period. This chart shows that investors continually reaffirmed the security's upward movement.

FIGURE 43

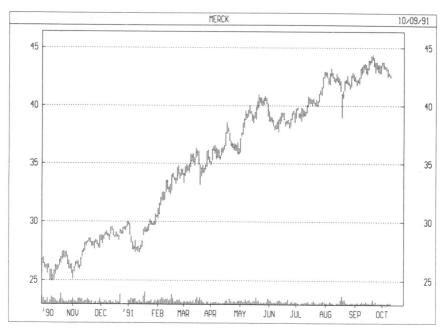

As shown in Figure 44, Disney's price also moved from around $25.00 to $45.00, but it did so in two significant moves. This shows that on two occasions investors believed the security's price would move higher. But following the first bidding war, a period of time had to pass before investors accepted the new prices and were ready to move them higher.

FIGURE 44

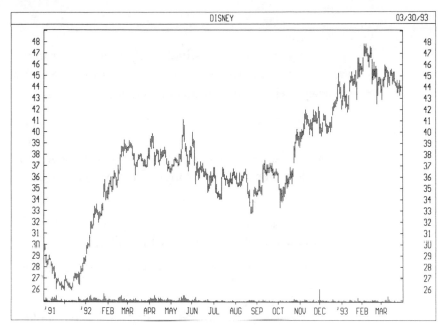

The pause after the rapid increase in Disney's price is a typical phenomenon. People have a difficult time accepting new prices suddenly, but will accept them over time. What once looked expensive may one day look cheap as expectations evolve.

This is an interesting aspect of point-and-figure charts (see page 233), because point-and-figure charts totally disregard the passage of time and only display changes in price.

A SAMPLE APPROACH

There are *many* technical analysis tools in this book. The most difficult part of technical analysis may be deciding which tools to use! Here is an approach you might try.

1. Determine the overall market condition.
    If you are trading equity-based securities (e.g., stocks), determine the trend in interest rates, the trend of the New York Stock Exchange, and the trend of investor sentiment (e.g., read

the newspaper). The object is to determine the overall trend of the market.

2. Pick the securities.

    I suggest that you pick the securities using either a company or industry you are familiar with, or the recommendation of a trusted analyst (either fundamental or technical).

3. Determine the overall trend of the security.

    Plot a 200-day (or 39-week) moving average of the security's closing price. The best buying opportunities occur when the security has just risen above this long-term moving average.

4. Pick your entry points.

    Buy and sell using your favorite indicator. However, only take positions that agree with overall market conditions.

Much of your success in technical analysis will come from experience. The goal isn't to find the holy grail of technical analysis, it is to reduce your risks (e.g., by trading with the overall trend) while capitalizing on opportunities (e.g., using your favorite in-dicator to time your trades). As you gain experience, you will make better, more informed, and more profitable investments.

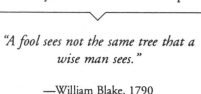

"A fool sees not the same tree that a wise man sees."

—William Blake, 1790

CONCLUSION

This concludes the Introduction to Technical Analysis. I suggest you refer to Part II while you continue to explore this exciting and potentially profitable pursuit.

A fitting conclusion to an introduction to technical analysis is a list of lessons I have learned, both from others and the hard way.

■ Don't compound your losses by averaging down (i.e., don't keep buying additional shares at lower prices). It is tempting to think that a loss "doesn't count" until the position is closed—but it does!

- Any time you own a security, ask yourself if you would buy it today. If you wouldn't buy it, you should consider selling it.

- Don't get distracted by oth-ers' investment prowess. Most investors only discuss their successes, threatening your focus and confidence.

"Opportunities flit by while we sit regretting the chances we have lost."

—Jerome K. Jerome, 1889

- Wise investments aren't made with Ouija boards, they are made using logical approaches that minimize risks and maximize opportunities.

- Master the basics. Most investors spend their time looking for easy money (which is not an easy search) instead of learning the key factors to security prices—supply and demand.

PART
TWO

REFERENCE

Part Two is a concise reference to a vast array of technical indicators and line studies.

The discussion on each tool includes an overview, an explanation of its interpretation, and an example of the indicator or line study in action. When space has permitted, I have also included a step-by-step explanation of the relevant calculations.

Most of these techniques can be applied to any type of security, including stocks, bonds, options, futures, mutual funds, and indices.

ABSOLUTE BREADTH INDEX

OVERVIEW

The Absolute Breadth Index (ABI) is a market momentum indicator that was developed by Norman G. Fosback.

The ABI shows how much activity, volatility, and change is taking place on the New York Stock Exchange while ignoring the direction prices are headed.

INTERPRETATION

You can think of the ABI as an "activity index." High readings indicate market activity and change, while low readings indicate lack of change.

In Fosback's book, *Stock Market Logic,* he indicates that historically, high values typically lead to higher prices three to 12 months later. Fosback found that a highly reliable variation of the ABI is to divide the weekly ABI by the total issues traded. A 10-week moving average of this value is then calculated. Readings above 40 percent are very bullish and readings below 15 percent are bearish.

EXAMPLE

The following chart shows the S&P 500 and a five-week moving average of the ABI. Strong rallies occurred every time the ABI's moving average rose above 450.

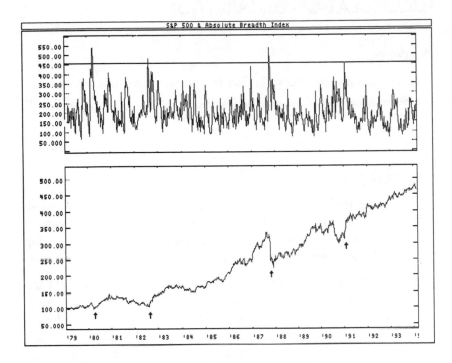

S&P 500 & Absolute Breadth Index

CALCULATION

The Absolute Breadth Index is calculated by taking the absolute value of the difference between NYSE Advancing Issues and NYSE Declining Issues.

ABS (Advancing Issues − Declining Issues)

Absolute value (i.e., ABS) means "regardless of sign." Thus, the absolute value of −100 is 100 and the absolute value of +100 is also 100.

ACCUMULATION/DISTRIBUTION

OVERVIEW

The Accumulation/Distribution is a momentum indicator that associates changes in price and volume. The indicator is based on the premise that the more volume that accompanies a price move, the more significant the price move.

INTERPRETATION

The Accumulation/Distribution is really a variation of the more popular On Balance Volume indicator (see page 207). Both of these indicators attempt to confirm changes in prices by comparing the volume associated with prices.

When the Accumulation/Distribution moves up, it shows that the security is being accumulated (i.e., bought), as most of the volume is associated with upward price movement. When the indicator moves down, it shows that the security is being distributed (i.e., sold), as most of the volume is associated with downward price movement.

Divergences (see page 35) between the Accumulation/Distribution and the security's price imply a change is imminent. When a divergence does occur, prices usually change to confirm the Accumulation/Distribution. For example, if the indicator is moving up and the security's price is going down, prices will probably reverse.

EXAMPLE

The following chart shows Battle Mountain Gold and its Accumulation/Distribution. Battle Mountain's price diverged as it reached new highs in late July while the indicator was falling. Prices then corrected to confirm the indicator's trend.

ACCUMULATION/DISTRIBUTION
IN A FALLING TREND

PRICES MAKING NEW HIGHS   PRICE CORRECTION

CALCULATION

A portion of each day's volume is added or subtracted from a cumulative total. The nearer the closing price is to the high for the day, the more volume added to the cumulative total. The nearer the closing price is to the low for the day, the more volume subtracted from the cumulative total. If the close is exactly between the high and low prices, nothing is added to the cumulative total.

$$\sum \left[\frac{(close - low) - (high - close)}{(high - low)} * volume \right]$$

ACCUMULATION SWING INDEX

OVERVIEW

The Accumulation Swing Index is a cumulative total of the Swing Index (see page 272). The Accumulation Swing Index was developed by Welles Wilder.

INTERPRETATION

Mr. Wilder said, "Somewhere amidst the maze of Open, High, Low, and Close prices is a phantom line that is the *real* market." The Accumulation Swing Index attempts to show this phantom line. Since the Accumulation Swing Index attempts to show the "real market," it closely resembles prices themselves. This allows you to use classic support/resistance analysis on the Index itself. Typical analysis involves looking for breakouts, new highs and lows, and divergences.

Wilder notes the following characteristics of the Accumulation Swing Index:

- It provides a numerical value that quantifies price swings.

- It defines short-term swing points.

- It cuts through the maze of high, low, and close prices and indicates the real strength and direction of the market.

EXAMPLE

The following chart shows corn and its Accumulation Swing Index. You can see that the breakouts of the price trendlines labeled A and B were confirmed by breakouts of the Accumulation Swing Index trendlines labeled A' and B'.

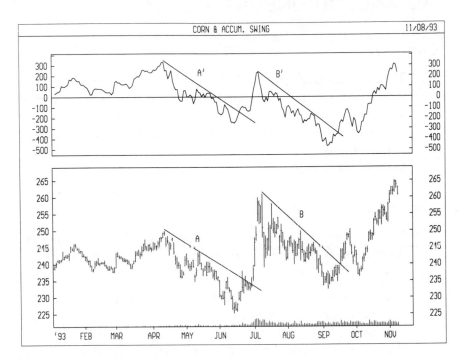

CALCULATION

The Accumulation Swing Index is a cumulative total of the Swing Index (see page 272). The Swing Index and the Accumulation Swing Index require opening prices.

Step-by-step instructions on calculating the Swing Index are provided in Wilder's book, *New Concepts in Technical Trading Systems*.

ADVANCE/DECLINE LINE

OVERVIEW

The Advance/Decline Line (A/D Line) is undoubtedly the most widely used measure of market breadth. It is a cumulative total of the Advancing-Declining Issues indicator (see page 61). When compared to the movement of a market index (e.g., Dow Jones Industrials, S&P 500) the A/D Line has proven to be an effective gauge of the stock market's strength.

INTERPRETATION

The A/D Line is helpful when measuring overall market strength. When more stocks are advancing than declining, the A/D Line moves up (and vice versa).

Many investors feel that the A/D Line shows market strength better than more commonly used indices such as the Dow Jones Industrial Average (DJIA) or the S&P 500 Index. By studying the trend of the A/D Line you can see if the market is in a rising or falling trend, if the trend is still intact, and how long the current trend has prevailed.

Another way to use the A/D Line is to look for a divergence (see page 35) between the DJIA (or a similar index) and the A/D Line. Often, an end to a bull market can be forecast when the A/D Line begins to round over while the DJIA is still trying to make new highs. Historically, when a divergence develops between the DJIA and the A/D Line, the DJIA has corrected and gone the direction of the A/D Line.

A military analogy is often used when discussing the relationship between the A/D Line and the DJIA. The analogy is that trouble looms when the generals lead (e.g., the DJIA is making new highs) and the troops refuse to follow (e.g., the A/D Line fails to make new highs).

EXAMPLE

The following chart shows the DJIA and the A/D Line. The DJIA was making new highs during the 12 months leading up to the 1987 crash. During this same period, the A/D Line was failing to reach new highs. This type of divergence, where the generals lead and the troops refuse to follow, usually results in the generals retreating in defeat, as happened in 1987.

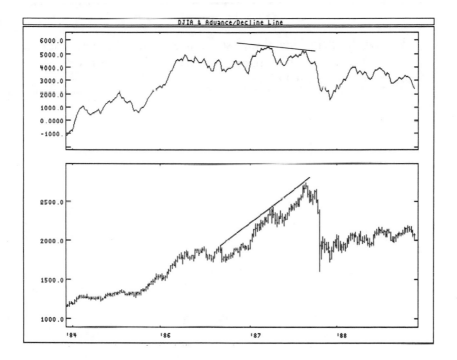

CALCULATION

The A/D Line is calculated by subtracting the number of stocks that declined in price for the day from the number of stocks that advanced, and then adding this value to a cumulative total.

Table 2 shows the calculation of the A/D Line.

TABLE 2

Date	Advancing	Declining	A-D	A/D Line
02/15/94	1,198	882	316	316
02/16/94	1,183	965	218	534
02/17/94	882	1,251	−369	165
02/18/94	706	1,411	−705	−540
02/22/94	1,139	1,003	136	−404

Because the A/D Line always starts at zero, the numeric value of the A/D Line is of little importance. What is important is the slope and pattern of the A/D Line.

ADVANCE/DECLINE RATIO

OVERVIEW

The Advance/Decline Ratio (A/D Ratio) shows the ratio of advancing issues to declining issues. It is calculated by dividing the number of advancing issues by the number of declining issues.

INTERPRETATION

The A/D Ratio is similar to the Advancing-Declining Issues (see page 61) in that it displays market breadth. But, where the Advancing-Declining Issues subtracts the advancing/declining values, the A/D Ratio divides the values. The advantage of the Ratio is that it remains constant regardless of the number of issues that are traded on the New York Stock Exchange (which has steadily increased).

A moving average of the A/D Ratio is often used as an overbought/oversold indicator. The higher the value, the more "excessive" the rally and the more likely a correction. Likewise, low readings imply an oversold market and suggest a technical rally.

Keep in mind, however, that markets that appear to be extremely overbought or oversold may stay that way for some time. When investing using overbought and oversold indicators, it is wise to wait for the prices to confirm your belief that a change is due before placing your trades.

Day-to-day fluctuations of the Advance/Decline Ratio are often eliminated by smoothing the ratio with a moving average.

EXAMPLE

The following chart shows the S&P 500 and a 15-day moving average of the A/D Ratio. You can see that prices usually declined after entering the overbought level above 1.25 ("sell" arrows) and that they usually rallied after entering the oversold level below 0.90 ("buy" arrows).

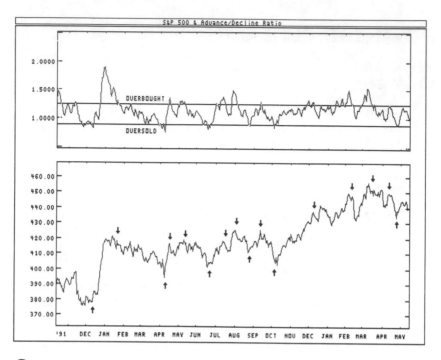

CALCULATION

The A/D Ratio is calculated by dividing the number of stocks that advanced in price for the day by the number of stocks that declined.

$$\frac{Advancing \ Issues}{Declining \ Issues}$$

Table 3 shows the calculation of the A/D Ratio.

TABLE 3

DATE	ADVANCING	DECLINING	A/D RATIO
02/15/94	1,198	882	1.3583
02/16/94	1,183	965	1.2259
02/17/94	882	1,251	0.7050
02/18/94	706	1,411	0.5004
02/22/94	1,139	1,003	1.1356

ADVANCING-DECLINING ISSUES

OVERVIEW

The Advancing-Declining Issues is a market momentum indicator that shows the difference between stocks listed on the New York Stock Exchange that advanced in price minus those that declined. As of this writing, about 2,500 issues trade each day on the NYSE.

The difference between the number of advancing and declining issues is the foundation of many market breadth indicators. These indicators include the Advance/Decline Line, Advance/Decline Ratio, Absolute Breadth Index, Breadth Thrust, McClellan Oscillator, and McClellan Summation Index. Indicators that use advancing and declining issues in their calculations are called market breadth indicators.

INTERPRETATION

The Advancing-Declining Issues indicator shows the difference between the number of advancing issues and the number of declining issues. Plotted by itself, this indicator helps to determine daily market strength. Strong up days generally show readings of more than +1,000. Very weak days have readings of less than −1,000.

I prefer to plot a 5- to 40-day exponential moving average of the Advancing-Declining Issues rather than the daily values themselves. The moving average creates an excellent short-term over-bought/oversold indicator. Both the Overbought/Oversold indicator (see page 220) and the McClellan Oscillator (see page 171) are created using moving averages of advancing minus declining issues.

EXAMPLE

The following chart shows the DJIA and a 40-day moving average of the Advancing-Declining Issues indicator. I drew "buy" arrows when the moving average rose above −50 and "sell" arrows when it fell below 125. Normally, I would use ±100, but the strong up-trend during this period caused the indicator to have an upward bias.

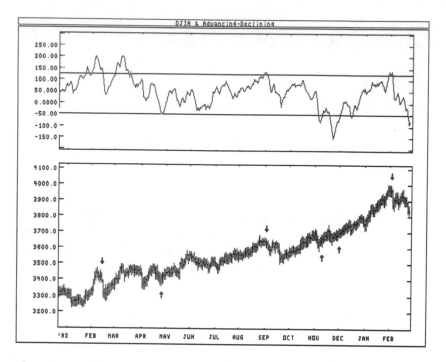

CALCULATION

The Advancing-Declining Issues is calculated simply by subtracting the number of declining issues from the number of advancing issues.

Advancing Issues – Declining Issues

Table 4 shows the calculation of the Advancing-Declining Issues.

TABLE 4

DATE	ADVANCING	DECLINING	A-D
02/15/94	1,198	882	316
02/16/94	1,183	965	218
02/17/94	882	1,251	−369
02/18/94	706	1,411	−705
02/22/94	1,139	1,003	136

ADVANCING, DECLINING, UNCHANGED VOLUME

OVERVIEW

Advancing, declining, and unchanged volume are all market momentum indicators. They reflect movement on the New York Stock Exchange in millions of shares.

Advancing volume is the total volume for all securities that advanced in price. Declining volume is the total volume for all securities that declined in price. And similarly, unchanged volume is the total volume for all securities that were unchanged in price.

INTERPRETATION

Numerous indicators have been developed using up and down volume indicators. These indicators include the Cumulative Volume Index, Negative Volume Index, Positive Volume Index, and the Upside/Downside Ratio. Charts of the advancing or declining volume can be used to look for volume divergences (where advancing volume increases but the market falls) to see if selling pressure is waning, to view daily trends, etc.

Due to the erratic fluctuations in advancing and declining volume, I suggest you smooth the indicators with a 3- to 10-day moving average.

EXAMPLE

The following chart shows the S&P 500 and a 10-day moving average of advancing volume. A bearish divergence developed as prices tried to rally (trendline A) while the advancing volume was declining (trendline B). If you only looked at the S&P 500, you might think the market was gaining strength. The Advancing Volume showed the true picture and prices were forced to correct.

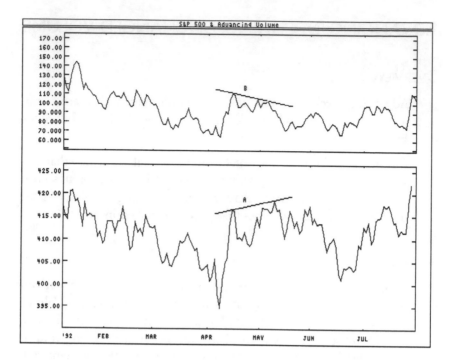

ANDREWS' PITCHFORK

OVERVIEW

Andrews' Pitchfork is a line study consisting of three parallel trend-lines based on three points you select. This tool was developed by Dr. Alan Andrews.

INTERPRETATION

The interpretation of a pitchfork is based on normal trendline support and resistance principles (see page 10).

EXAMPLE

The following chart of Xerox shows an Andrews' Pitchfork. The pitchfork was displayed by selecting the three points shown. You can see how prices tended to "walk along" the trendlines.

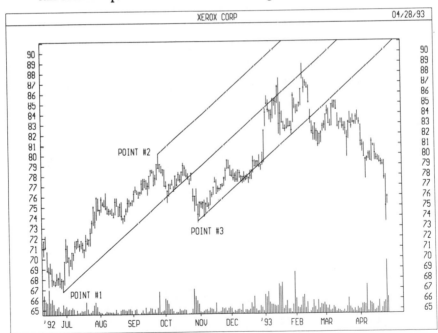

CALCULATION

The first trendline begins at the leftmost point selected (either a major peak or trough) and is drawn so that it passes directly between the two rightmost points. This line is the "handle" of the pitchfork. The second and third trendlines are then drawn beginning at the two rightmost points (a major peak and a major trough) and are drawn parallel to the first line. These lines are the "tines" of the pitchfork.

ARMS INDEX

OVERVIEW

The Arms Index is a market indicator that shows the relationship between the number of stocks that increase or decrease in price (advancing/declining issues) and the volume associated with stocks that increase or decrease in price (advancing/declining volume). It is calculated by dividing the Advance/Decline Ratio (see page 59) by the Upside/Downside Ratio (see page 296).

The Arms Index was developed by Richard W. Arms, Jr. in 1967. Over the years, the index has been referred to by a number of different names. When *Barron's* published the first article on the indicator in 1967, they called it the Short-Term Trading Index. It has also been known as TRIN (an acronym for TRading INdex), MKDS, and STKS.

INTERPRETATION

The Arms Index is primarily a short-term trading tool. The Index shows whether volume is flowing into advancing or declining stocks. If more volume is associated with advancing stocks than declining stocks, the Arms Index will be less than 1.0; if more volume is associated with declining stocks, the Index will be greater than 1.0.

The Index is usually smoothed with a moving average. I suggest using a 4-day moving average for short-term analysis, a 21-day moving average for intermediate-term, and a 55-day moving average for longer-term analysis.

Normally, the Arms Index is considered bullish when it is below 1.0 and bearish when it is above 1.0. However, the Index seems to work most effectively as an overbought/oversold indicator. When the indicator drops to extremely overbought levels, it is foretelling a selling opportunity. When it rises to extremely oversold levels, a buying opportunity is approaching.

What constitutes an "extremely" overbought or oversold level depends on the length of the moving average used to smooth the indicator and on market conditions. Table 5 shows typical over-bought and oversold levels.

TABLE 5

Moving Average	Overbought	Oversold
4-day	0.70	1.25
21-day	0.85	1.10
55-day	0.90	1.05

EXAMPLE

The following chart contains a 21-day moving average of the Arms Index and the New York Stock Exchange Index. Horizontal lines are drawn at the oversold level of 1.08 and at the overbought level of 0.85. I drew "buy" arrows when the Arms Index peaked above 1.08 and "sell" arrows when the Index bottomed below 0.85. In most of the cases the arrows occur at, or one day before, significant changes in price.

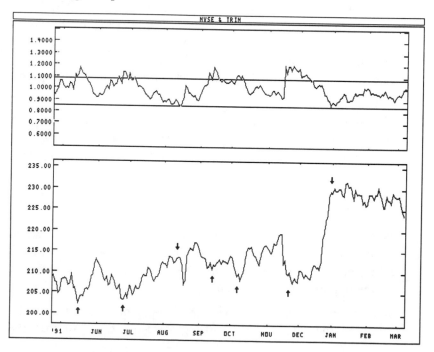

CALCULATION

The Arms Index is calculated by first dividing the number of stocks that advanced in price by the number of stocks that declined in price to determine the Advance/Decline Ratio (see page 59). Next, the volume of advancing stocks is divided by the volume of declining stocks to determine the Upside/Downside Ratio (see page 296). Finally, the Advance/Decline Ratio is divided by the Upside/Downside Ratio.

$$\frac{Advancing \ \ Issues \ / Declining \ \ Issues}{Advancing \ \ Volume \ / Declining \ \ Volume}$$

AVERAGE TRUE RANGE

OVERVIEW

The Average True Range (ATR) is a measure of volatility. It was introduced by Welles Wilder in his book, *New Concepts in Technical Trading Systems,* and has since been used as a component of many indicators and trading systems.

INTERPRETATION

Wilder has found that high ATR values often occur at market bottoms following a "panic" sell-off. Low Average True Range values are often found during extended sideways periods, such as those found at tops and after consolidation periods.

The Average True Range can be interpreted using the same techniques that are used with the other volatility indicators. Refer to the discussion on Standard Deviation (page 264) for additional information on volatility interpretation.

EXAMPLE

The following chart shows McDonald's and its Average True Range. This is a good example of high volatility as prices bottom (points A and A') and low volatility as prices consolidate prior to a breakout (points B and B').

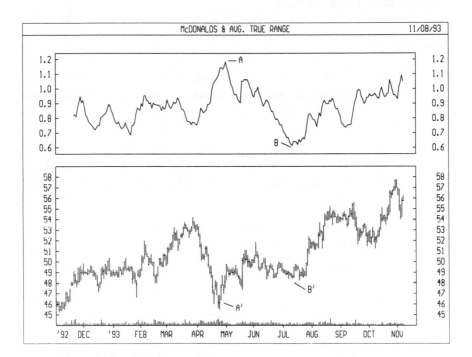

CALCULATION

The True Range indicator is the greatest of the following:

■ The distance from today's high to today's low.

■ The distance from yesterday's close to today's high.

■ The distance from yesterday's close to today's low.

The Average True Range is a moving average (typically 14 days) of the True Ranges.

BOLLINGER BANDS

OVERVIEW

Bollinger Bands are similar to moving average envelopes (see page 129). The difference between Bollinger Bands and envelopes is that envelopes are plotted at a fixed percentage above and below a moving average, whereas Bollinger Bands are plotted at standard deviation levels (see page 264) above and below a moving average. Since standard deviation is a measure of volatility, the bands are self-adjusting, widening during volatile markets and contracting during calmer periods.

Bollinger Bands were created by John Bollinger.

INTERPRETATION

Bollinger Bands are usually displayed on top of security prices, but they can be displayed on an indicator. These comments refer to bands displayed on prices.

As with moving average envelopes, the basic interpretation of Bollinger Bands is that prices tend to stay within the upper and lower band. The distinctive characteristic of Bollinger Bands is that the spacing between the bands varies based on the volatility of the prices. During periods of extreme price changes (i.e., high volatility), the bands widen to become more forgiving. During periods of stagnant pricing (i.e., low volatility), the bands narrow to contain prices.

Mr. Bollinger notes the following characteristics of Bollinger Bands:

- Sharp price changes tend to occur after the bands tighten, as volatility lessens.

- When prices move outside the bands, a continuation of the current trend is implied.

- Bottoms and tops made outside the bands followed by bottoms and tops made inside the bands call for reversals in the trend.

- A move that originates at one band tends to go all the way to the other band. This observation is useful when projecting price targets.

EXAMPLE

The following chart shows Bollinger Bands on Exxon's prices. The Bands were calculated using a 20-day exponential moving average and are spaced two deviations apart.

The bands were at their widest when prices were volatile during April. They narrowed when prices entered a consolidation period later in the year. The narrowing of the bands increases the probability of a sharp breakout in prices. The longer prices remain within the narrow bands the more likely a price breakout.

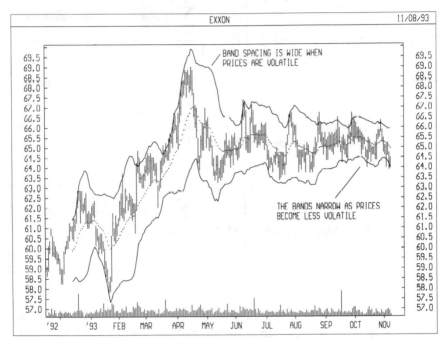

CALCULATION

Bollinger Bands are displayed as three bands. The middle band is a normal moving average. In the following formula, "n" is the number of time periods in the moving average (e.g., 20 days).

$$Middle\ Band = \frac{\sum_{j=1}^{n} Close_j}{n}$$

The upper band is the same as the middle band, but it is shifted up by the number of standard deviations (e.g., two deviations). In this next formula, "D" is the number of standard deviations.

$$Upper\ Band\ =\ Middle\ Band\ +\ \left[D * \sqrt{\frac{\sum_{j=1}^{n} (Close_j - Middle\ Band)^2}{n}} \right]$$

The lower band is the moving average shifted down by the same number of standard deviations (i.e., "D").

$$Lower\ Band\ =\ Middle\ Band\ -\ \left[D * \sqrt{\frac{\sum_{j=1}^{n} (Close_j - Middle\ Band)^2}{n}} \right]$$

Mr. Bollinger recommends using 20 for the number of periods in the moving average, calculating the moving average using the "simple" method (as shown in the formula for the middle band), and using 2 standard deviations. He has also found that moving averages of less than 10 periods do not work very well.

BREADTH THRUST

OVERVIEW

The Breadth Thrust indicator is a market momentum indicator. It was developed by Dr. Martin Zweig. The Breadth Thrust is calculated by dividing a 10-day exponential moving average of the number of advancing issues by the number of advancing plus declining issues.

INTERPRETATION

A Breadth Thrust occurs when, during a 10-day period, the Breadth Thrust indicator rises from below 40 percent to above 61.5 percent. A "Thrust" indicates that the stock market has rapidly changed from an oversold condition to one of strength, but has not yet become overbought.

According to Dr. Zweig, there have only been 14 Breadth Thrusts since 1945. The average gain following these 14 Thrusts was 24.6 percent in an average time frame of 11 months. Dr. Zweig also points out that most bull markets begin with a Breadth Thrust.

EXAMPLE

The following chart shows the S&P 500 and the Breadth Thrust indicator. Horizontal lines are drawn on the Breadth Thrust indicator at 40.0 percent and 61.5 percent. Remember that a Thrust occurs when the indicator moves from below 40 percent to above 61.5 percent during a 10-day period.

On December 18, 1984, I wrote the following comment regarding the Breadth Thrust indicator in a software manual:

"At the time this discussion on the Breadth Thrust is being written (12/18/84), the NYSE has gained only 1.6 percent since the 'Thrust.' If the market fails to go higher in the next 6 to 12 months, it will be the first false signal generated by the Breadth Thrust indicator in 39 years! With historical average gains of almost 25 percent, we feel the odds are in our favor when we go with the Thrust."

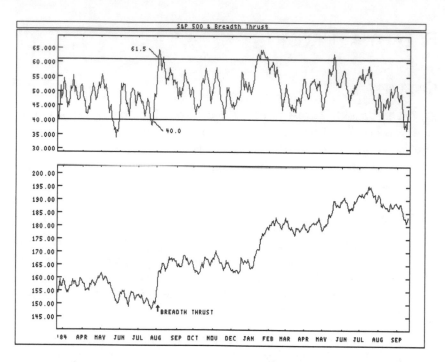

As shown in the example, the NYSE did in fact go higher in the ensuing months. Twelve months after the Thrust occurred, the NYSE was up 21.6 percent. Twenty-one months after the Thrust occurred, the NYSE was up a whopping 51 percent. Trust the next Thrust.

CALCULATION

The Breadth Thrust is a 10-day simple moving average of the following:

$$\frac{Advancing\ Issues}{(Advancing\ Issues + Declining\ Issues)}$$

BULL/BEAR RATIO

OVERVIEW

Each week a poll of investment advisors is taken and published by Investor's Intelligence of New Rochelle, New York. Investment advisors are tracked as to whether they are bullish, bearish, or neutral on the stock market. The Bull/Bear Ratio shows the relationship between the bullish and bearish advisors.

INTERPRETATION

The Bull/Bear Ratio is a market sentiment indicator. Dr. Martin Zweig sums up sentiment indicators in his book *Winning on Wall Street* by saying, "Beware of the crowd when the crowd is too one-sided." Extreme optimism on the part of the public and even professionals almost always coincides with market tops. Extreme pessimism almost always coincides with market bottoms.

High readings of the Bull/Bear Ratio are bearish (there are too many bulls) and low readings are bullish (there are not enough bulls). In almost every case, extremely high or low readings have coincided with market tops or bottoms. Historically, readings above 60 percent have indicated extreme optimism (which is bearish for the market) and readings below 40 percent have indicated extreme pessimism (which is bullish for the market).

EXAMPLE

The following chart shows the Bull/Bear Ratio and the S&P 500. "Buy" arrows were drawn on the S&P 500 when the advisors were extremely bearish and "sell" arrows were drawn when advisors were extremely bullish.

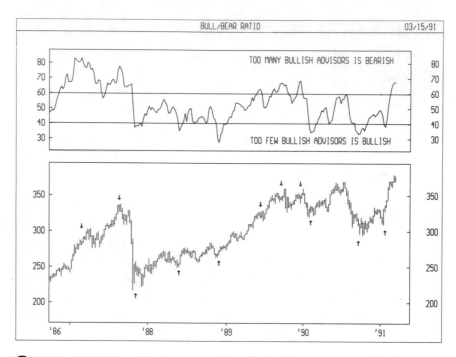

TOO MANY BULLISH ADVISORS IS BEARISH

TOO FEW BULLISH ADVISORS IS BULLISH

CALCULATION

The Bull/Bear Ratio is calculated by dividing the number of bullish advisors by the number of bullish plus bearish advisors. The number of neutral advisors is ignored.

$$\frac{Bullish\ Advisors}{Bullish\ Advisors\ +\ Bearish\ Advisors} * 100$$

CANDLESTICKS, JAPANESE

OVERVIEW

In the 1600s, the Japanese developed a method of technical analysis to analyze the price of rice contracts. This technique is called candlestick charting. Steven Nison is credited with popularizing candlestick charting and has become recognized as the leading expert on the interpretation of candlestick charts.

Candlestick charts display the open, high, low, and closing prices in a format similar to a modern-day bar chart, but in a manner that extenuates the relationship between the opening and closing prices. Candlestick charts are simply a new way of looking at prices; they don't involve any calculations.

Each candlestick represents one period (e.g., day) of data. Figure 45 displays the elements of a candle.

FIGURE 45

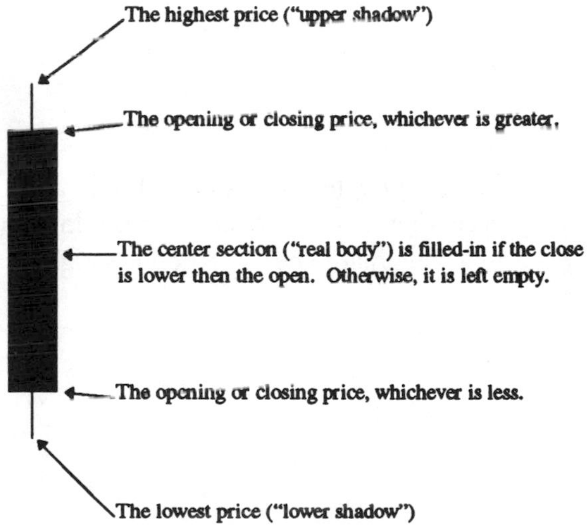

The highest price ("upper shadow")

The opening or closing price, whichever is greater.

The center section ("real body") is filled-in if the close is lower then the open. Otherwise, it is left empty.

The opening or closing price, whichever is less.

The lowest price ("lower shadow")

INTERPRETATION

I have met investors who are attracted to candlestick charts by their mystique—maybe they are the "long-forgotten Asian secret" to investment analysis. Other investors are turned off by this mystique—they are only charts, right? Regardless of your feelings about the heritage of candlestick charting, I strongly encourage you to explore their use. Candlestick charts dramatically illustrate changes in the underlying supply/demand lines.

Because candlesticks display the relationship between the open, high, low, and closing prices, they cannot be displayed on securities that only have closing prices, nor were they intended to be displayed on securities that lack opening prices. If you want to display a candlestick chart on a security that does not have opening prices, I suggest that you use the previous day's closing prices in place of opening prices. This technique can create candlestick lines and patterns that are unusual, but valid.

The interpretation of candlestick charts is based primarily on patterns. The most popular patterns are explained on the following pages.

BULLISH PATTERNS

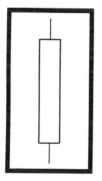

Long white (empty) line. This is a bullish line. It occurs when prices open near the low and close significantly higher near the period's high.

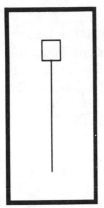

Hammer. This is a bullish line if it occurs after a significant downtrend. If the line occurs after a significant uptrend, it is called a Hanging Man (see page 82). A Hammer is identified by a small real body (i.e., a small range between the open and closing prices) and a long lower shadow (i.e., the low is significantly lower than the open, high, and close). The body can be empty or filled in.

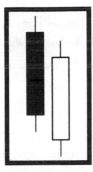

Piercing line. This is a bullish pattern and the opposite of a dark cloud cover (see page 82). The first line is a long black line (see page 82) and the second line is a long white line (see page 80). The second line opens lower than the first line's low, but it closes more than halfway above the first line's real body.

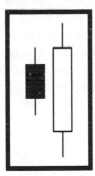

Bullish engulfing lines. This pattern is strongly bullish if it occurs after a significant downtrend (i.e., it acts as a reversal pattern). It occurs when a small bearish (filled-in) line is engulfed by a large bullish (empty) line.

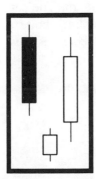

Morning star. This is a bullish pattern signifying a potential bottom. The "star" (see page 84) indicates a possible reversal and the bullish (empty) line confirms this. The star can be empty or filled in.

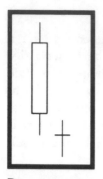

Bullish doji star. A "star" (see page 84) indicates a reversal and a doji indicates indecision. Thus, this pattern usually indicates a reversal following an indecisive period. You should wait for a confirmation (e.g., as in the morning star, above) before trading a doji star. The first line can be empty or filled in.

Bearish patterns

Long black (filled-in) line. This is a bearish line. It occurs when prices open near the high and close significantly lower near the period's low.

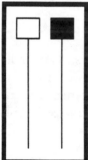

Hanging Man. These lines are bearish if they occur after a significant uptrend. If this pattern occurs after a significant downtrend, it is called a Hammer (see page 81). They are identified by small real bodies (i.e., a small range between the open and closing prices) and a long lower shadow (i.e., the low was significantly lower than the open, high, and close). The bodies can be empty or filled in.

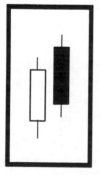

Dark cloud cover. This is a bearish pattern. The pattern is more significant if the second line's body is below the center of the previous line's body (as illustrated).

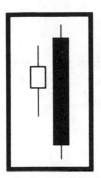

Bearish engulfing lines. This pattern is strongly bearish if it occurs after a significant uptrend (i.e., it acts as a reversal pattern). It occurs when a small bullish (empty) line is engulfed by a large bearish (filled-in) line.

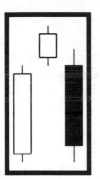

Evening star. This is a bearish pattern signifying a potential top. The "star" (see page 84) indicates a possible reversal and the bearish (filled-in) line confirms this. The star can be empty or filled in.

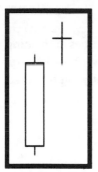

Doji star. A star indicates a reversal and a doji indicates indecision. Thus, this pattern usually indicates a reversal following an indecisive period. You should wait for a confirmation (e.g., as in the evening star illustration) before trading a doji star.

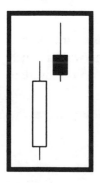

Shooting star. This pattern suggests a minor reversal when it appears after a rally. The star's body must appear near the low price and the line should have a long upper shadow.

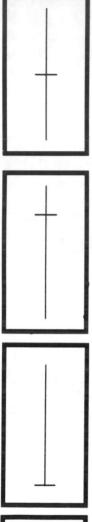

Long-legged doji. This line often signifies a turning point. It occurs when the open and close are the same, and the range between the high and low is relatively large.

Dragonfly doji. This line also signifies a turning point. It occurs when the open and close are the same, and the low is significantly lower than the open, high, and closing prices.

Gravestone doji. This line also signifies a turning point. It occurs when the open, close, and low are the same, and the high is significantly higher than the open, low, and closing prices.

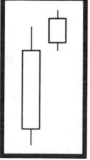

Star. Stars indicate reversals. A star is a line with a small real body that occurs after a line with a much larger real body, where the real bodies do not overlap. The shadows may overlap.

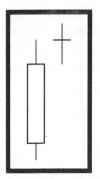

Doji star. A star indicates a reversal and a doji indicates indecision. Thus, this pattern usually indicates a reversal following an indecisive period. You should wait for a confirmation (e.g., as in the evening star illustration) before trading a doji star.

Neutral Patterns

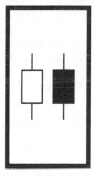

Spinning tops. These are neutral lines. They occur when the distance between the high and low, and the distance between the open and close, are relatively small.

Doji. This line implies indecision. The security opened and closed at the same price. These lines can appear in several different patterns.

Double doji lines (two adjacent doji lines) imply that a forceful move will follow a breakout from the current indecision.

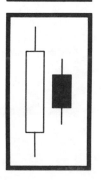

Harami ("pregnant" in English). This pattern indicates a decrease in momentum. It occurs when a line with a small body falls within the area of a larger body. In this example, a bullish (empty) line with a long body is followed by a weak bearish (filled-in) line. This implies a decrease in the bullish momentum.

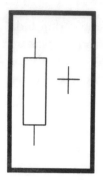

Harami cross. This pattern also indicates a decrease in momentum. The pattern is similar to a harami, except the second line is a doji (signifying indecision).

EXAMPLE

The following chart of corn illustrates several Japanese candlestick patterns and principles.

You can see that advancing prices are usually accompanied by empty lines (prices opened low and closed higher) and that declines are accompanied by filled-in lines (prices opened high and closed lower).

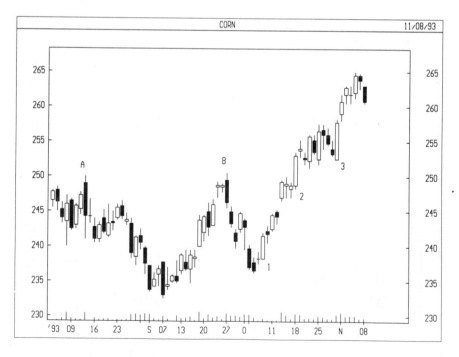

Bearish engulfing lines occurred at points A and B (and prices subsequently moved lower). Bullish white lines occurred at points 1, 2, and 3 (as prices moved higher).

CANSLIM

OVERVIEW

CANSLIM is an acronym for a stock market investment method developed by William O'Neil. O'Neil is the founder and chairman of *Investor's Business Daily,* a national business newspaper. He also heads an investment research organization, William O'Neil & Company, Inc.

Drawing from his study of the greatest money-making stocks from 1953 to 1985, O'Neil developed a set of common characteristics that each of these stocks possessed. The key characteristics to focus on are captured in the acronym CANSLIM.

C urrent quarterly earnings per share
A nnual earnings growth
N ew products, new managements, new highs
S hares outstanding
L eading industry
I nstitutional sponsorship
M arket direction

Although not strictly a technical analysis tool, the CANSLIM approach combines worthy technical and fundamental concepts. The CANSLIM approach is covered in detail in O'Neil's book, *How To Make Money in Stocks.*

INTERPRETATION

The following text summarizes each of the seven components of the CANSLIM method.

CURRENT QUARTERLY EARNINGS

Earnings per share (EPS) for the most recent quarter should be up at least 20 percent when compared to the same quarter for the previous year (e.g., first quarter of 1993 to the first quarter of 1994).

ANNUAL EARNINGS GROWTH

Earnings per share over the last five years should be increasing at the rate of at least 15 percent per year. Preferably, the EPS should increase each year. However, a single year setback is acceptable if the EPS quickly recovers and moves back into new high territory.

NEW PRODUCTS, NEW MANAGEMENT, NEW HIGHS

A dramatic increase in a stock's price typically coincides with something "new." This could be a new product or service, a new CEO, a new technology, or even new high stock prices.

One of O'Neil's most surprising conclusions from his research is contrary to what many investors feel to be prudent. Instead of adhering to the old stock market maxim, "buy low and sell high," O'Neil would say, "buy high and sell higher." O'Neil's research concluded that the ideal time to purchase a stock is when it breaks into new high territory after going through a 2- to 15-month consolidation period. Some of the most dramatic increases follow such a breakout, due possibly to the lack of resistance (i.e., sellers).

SHARES OUTSTANDING

More than 95 percent of the stocks in O'Neil's study of the greatest stock market winners had less than 25 million shares outstanding. Using the simple principles of supply and demand (see page 16), restricting the shares outstanding forces the supply line to shift upward, which results in higher prices.

A huge amount of buying (i.e., demand) is required to move a stock with 400 million shares outstanding. However, only a moderate amount of buying is required to propel a stock with only 4 to 5 million shares outstanding (particularly if a large amount is held by corporate insiders).

LEADER

Although there is never a "satisfaction guaranteed" label attached to a stock, O'Neil found that you could significantly increase your chances of a profitable investment if you purchase a leading stock in a leading industry.

He also found that winning stocks are usually outperforming the majority of stocks in the overall market as well.

INSTITUTIONAL SPONSORSHIP

The biggest source of supply and demand comes from institutional buyers (e.g., mutual funds, banks, insurance companies). A stock does not require a large number of institutional sponsors, but institutional sponsors certainly give the stock a vote of approval. As a rule of thumb, O'Neil looks for stocks that have at least 3 to 10 institutional sponsors with better-than-average performance records.

However, too much sponsorship can be harmful. Once a stock has become "institutionalized" it may be too late. If 70 to 80 percent of a stock's outstanding shares are owned by institutions, the well may have run dry. The result of excessive institutional ownership can translate into excessive selling if bad news strikes.

O'Neil feels the ideal time to purchase a stock is when it has just become discovered by several quality institutional sponsors, but before it becomes so popular that it appears on every institution's hot list.

MARKET DIRECTION

This is the most important element in the formula. Even the best stocks can lose money if the general market goes into a slump. Approximately 75 percent of all stocks move with the general market. This means that you can pick stocks that meet all the other criteria perfectly, yet if you fail to determine the direction of the general market, your stocks will probably perform poorly.

Market indicators (see page 36) are designed to help you determine the conditions of the overall market. O'Neil says, "Learn to interpret a daily price and volume chart of the market averages. If you do, you can't get too far off the track. You really won't need much else unless you want to argue with the trend of the market."

CHAIKIN OSCILLATOR

OVERVIEW

Marc Chaikin developed a new volume indicator, extending the work done by his predecessors, Joseph Granville and Larry Williams. The Chaikin Oscillator is a moving average oscillator based on the Accumulation/Distribution indicator (see page 52).

INTERPRETATION

The following discussion of volume accumulation/distribution interpretation, written by Marc Chaikin, is reprinted here with his permission:

"Technical analysis of both market averages and individual stocks must include volume studies in order to give the technician a true picture of the internal dynamics of a given market. Volume analysis helps in identifying internal strengths and weaknesses that exist under the cover of price action. Very often, volume divergences versus price movement are the only clues to an important reversal that is about to take place. While volume has always been mentioned by technicians as important, little effective volume work was done until Joseph Granville and Larry Williams began to look at volume versus price in the late 1960s in a more creative way.

For many years it had been accepted that volume and price normally rose and fell together, but when this relationship changed, the price action should be examined for a possible change of trend. The Granville OBV concept which views the total volume on an up day as accumulation and the total volume on a down day as distribution is a decent one, but much too simplistic to be of value. The reason is that there are too many important tops and bottoms, both short-term and intermediate-term, where OBV confirms the price extreme. However, when an OBV line gives a divergence signal versus a price extreme, it can be a valuable technical signal and usually triggers a reversal in price.

Larry Williams took the OBV concept and improved on it. In order to determine whether there was accumulation or distribution in the market or an individual stock on a given day, Granville compared the closing price to the previous close, whereas Williams compared the closing price to the opening price. He [Williams] created a cumulative line by adding a percentage of total volume to the line if the close was higher than the opening and subtracting a percentage of the total volume if the close was lower than its opening price. The accumulation/distribution line improved results dramatically over the classic OBV approach to volume divergences.

Williams then took this one step further in analyzing the Dow Jones Industrials by creating an oscillator of the accumulation/distribution line for even better buy and sell signals. In the early 1970s, however, the opening price for stocks was eliminated from the daily newspaper and Williams' formula became difficult to compute without many daily calls to a stockbroker with a quote machine. Because of this void, I created the Chaikin Oscillator substituting the average price of the day for Williams' opening and took the approach one step further by applying the oscillator to stocks and commodities. The Chaikin Oscillator is an excellent tool for generating buy and sell signals when its action is compared to price movement. I believe it is a significant improvement over the work that preceded it.

The premise behind my oscillator is three-fold. The first premise is that if a stock or market average closes above its midpoint for the day (as defined by [high + low] / 2), then there was accumulation on that day. The closer a stock or average closes to its high, the more accumulation there was. Conversely, if a stock closes below its midpoint for the day, there was distribution on that day. The closer a stock closes to its low, the more distribution there was.

The second premise is that a healthy advance is accompanied by rising volume and a strong volume accumulation. Since volume is the fuel that powers rallies, it follows that lagging volume on rallies is a sign of less fuel available to move stocks higher.

Conversely, declines are usually accompanied by low volume, but end with panic-like liquidation on the part of institutional investors. Thus, we look for a pickup in volume and then lower-lows on reduced volume with some accumulation before a valid bottom can develop.

The third premise is that by using the Chaikin Oscillator, you can monitor the flow of volume into and out of the market. Comparing this flow to price action can help identify tops and bottoms, both short-term and intermediate-term.

Since no technical approach works all the time, I suggest using the oscillator along with other technical indicators to avoid problems. I favor using a price envelope (see page 129) around a 21-day moving average and an overbought/oversold oscillator together with the Chaikin Oscillator for the best short- and intermediate-term technical signals.

The most important signal generated by the Chaikin Oscillator occurs when prices reach a new high or new low for a swing, particularly at an overbought or oversold level, and the oscillator fails to exceed its previous extreme reading and then reverses direction.

1. Signals in the direction of the intermediate-term trend are more reliable than those against the trend.

2. A confirmed high or low does not imply any further price action in that direction. I view that as a non-event.

A second way to use the Chaikin Oscillator is to view a change of direction in the oscillator as a buy or sell signal, but only in the direction of the trend. For example, if we say that a stock that is above its 90-day moving average of price is in an uptrend, then an upturn of the oscillator while in negative territory would constitute a buy signal only if the stock were above its 90-day moving average—not below it.

A downturn of the oscillator while in positive territory (above zero) would be a sell signal if the stock were below its 90-day moving average of closing prices."

EXAMPLE

The following chart shows Eastman Kodak and the Chaikin Oscillator. Bearish divergences (where prices increased to new highs while the Oscillator was falling) occurred at points A and B. These divergences were warnings of the sell-offs that followed.

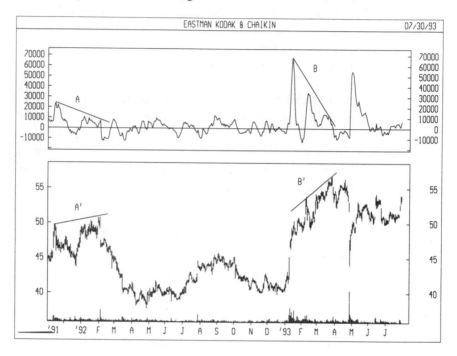

CALCULATION

The Chaikin Oscillator is created by subtracting a 10-period exponential moving average of the Accumulation/Distribution Line (see page 52) from a three-period exponential moving average of the Accumulation/Distribution Line.

COMMODITY CHANNEL INDEX

OVERVIEW

The Commodity Channel Index (CCI) measures the variation of a security's price from its statistical mean. High values show that prices are unusually high compared to average prices, whereas low values indicate that prices are unusually low. Contrary to its name, the CCI can be used effectively on any type of security, not just commodities.

The CCI was developed by Donald Lambert.

INTERPRETATION

There are two basic methods of interpreting the CCI: looking for divergences and as an overbought/oversold indicator.

- A divergence (see page 35) occurs when the security's prices are making new highs while the CCI is failing to surpass its previous highs. This classic divergence is usually followed by a correction in the security's price.

- The CCI typically oscillates between ±100. To use the CCI as an overbought/oversold indicator, readings above +100 imply an overbought condition (and a pending price correction) while readings below -100 imply an oversold condition (and a pending rally).

EXAMPLE

The following chart shows the British pound and its 14-day CCI. A bullish divergence occurred at point A (prices were declining as the CCI was advancing). Prices subsequently rallied. A bearish divergence occurred at point B (prices were advancing while the CCI was declining). Prices corrected. Note too, that each of these divergences occurred at extreme levels (i.e., above +100 or below -100) making them even more significant.

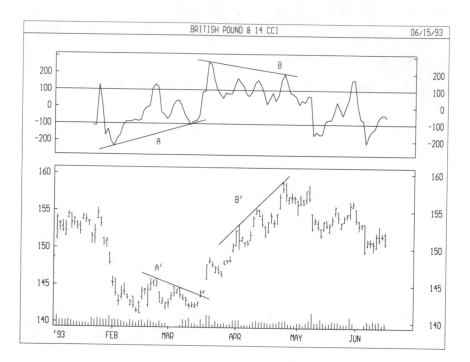

CALCULATION

A complete explanation of the CCI calculation is beyond the scope of this book. The following are basic steps involved in the calculation:

1. Add each period's high, low, and close and divide this sum by 3. This is the typical price (see page 291).

2. Calculate an n-period simple moving average of the typical prices computed in Step 1.

3. For each of the prior n-periods, subtract today's Step 2 value from Step 1's value n days ago. For example, if you were calculating a five-day CCI, you would perform five subtractions using today's Step 2 value.

4. Calculate an n-period simple moving average of the absolute values of each of the results in Step 3.

5. Multiply the value in Step 4 by 0.015.

6. Subtract the value from Step 2 from the value in Step 1.

7. Divide the value in Step 6 by the value in Step 5.

Further details on the contents and interpretation of the CCI can be found in an article by Donald Lambert that appeared in the October 1980 issue of *Commodities* (now known as *Futures*) magazine.

COMMODITY SELECTION INDEX

OVERVIEW

The Commodity Selection Index (CSI) is a momentum indicator. It was developed by Welles Wilder and is presented in his book *New Concepts in Technical Trading Systems.*

The name of the index reflects its primary purpose—that is, to help select commodities suitable for short-term trading.

INTERPRETATION

A high CSI rating indicates that the commodity has strong trending and volatility characteristics. The trending characteristics are brought out by the Directional Movement factor (see page 114) in the calculation—the volatility characteristic by the Average True Range factor (see page 70).

Wilder's approach is to trade commodities with high CSI values (relative to other commodities). Because these commodities are highly volatile, they have the potential to make the "most money in the shortest period of time." High CSI values imply trending characteristics, which makes it easier to trade the security.

The Commodity Selection Index is designed for short-term traders who can handle the risks associated with highly volatile markets.

EXAMPLE

The following chart shows the Japanese yen and its 14-day CSI. Strong volatility and strong trends result in high CSI values at points A and B.

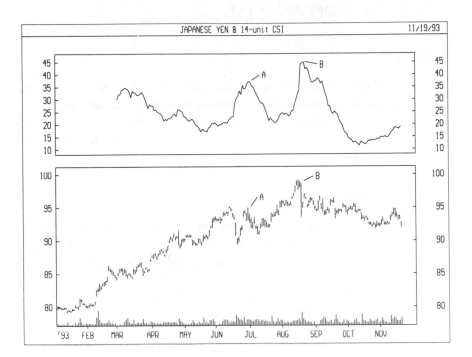

CALCULATION

It is beyond the scope of this book to provide full calculation details on the Commodity Selection Index. It is calculated using the ADXR component of the Directional Movement indicator (see page 114). Wilder's book *New Concepts in Technical Trading Systems* contains detailed information on the calculation of the CSI.

CORRELATION ANALYSIS

OVERVIEW

Correlation analysis measures the relationship between two items, for example, a security's price and an indicator. The resulting value (called the "correlation coefficient") shows if changes in one item (e.g., an indicator) will result in changes in the other item (e.g., the security's price).

INTERPRETATION

When comparing the correlation between two items, one item is called the "dependent" item and the other the "independent" item. The goal is to see if a change in the independent item (which is usually an indicator) will result in a change in the dependent item (usually a security's price). This information helps you understand an indicator's predictive abilities.

The correlation coefficient can range between ±1.0 (plus or minus one). A coefficient of +1.0, a "perfect positive correlation," means that changes in the independent item will result in an identical change in the dependent item (e.g., a change in the indicator will result in an identical change in the security's price). A coefficient of −1.0, a "perfect negative correlation," means that changes in the independent item will result in an identical change in the dependent item, but the change will be in the opposite direction. A coefficient of zero means there is no relationship between the two items and that a change in the independent item will have no effect in the dependent item.

A low correlation coefficient (e.g., less than ±0.10) suggests that the relationship between two items is weak or nonexistent. A high correlation coefficient (i.e., closer to plus or minus 1) indicates that the dependent variable (e.g., the security's price) will usually change when the independent variable (e.g., an indicator) changes.

The direction of the dependent variable's change depends on the sign of the coefficient. If the coefficient is a positive number, then the dependent variable will move in the same direction as the independent variable; if the coefficient is negative, then the dependent variable will move in the opposite direction of the independent variable.

You can use correlation analysis in two basic ways: to determine the predictive ability of an indicator and to determine the correlation between two securities.

When comparing the correlation between an indicator and a security's price, a high positive coefficient (e.g., more than +0.70) tells you that a change in the indicator will usually predict a change in the security's price. A high negative correlation (e.g., less than –0.70) tells you that when the indicator changes, the security's price will usually move in the opposite direction. Remember, a low (e.g., close to zero) coefficient indicates that the relationship between the security's price and the indicator is not significant.

Correlation analysis is also valuable in gauging the relationship between two securities. Often, one security's price "leads" or predicts the price of another security. For example, the correlation coefficient of gold versus the dollar shows a strong negative relationship. This means that an increase in the dollar usually predicts a decrease in the price of gold.

EXAMPLE

The following chart shows the relationship between corn and live hogs. The high correlation values show that, except during brief periods in February and May, there is a strong relationship between the price of these items (i.e., when the price of corn changes, the price of live hogs also moves in the same direction).

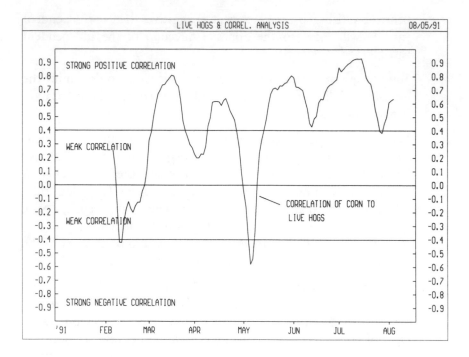

CUMULATIVE VOLUME INDEX

OVERVIEW

The Cumulative Volume Index (CVI) is a market momentum indicator that shows whether money is flowing into or out of the stock market. It is calculated by subtracting the volume of declining stocks from the volume of advancing stocks, and then adding this value to a running total. Advancing, declining, and unchanged volume are discussed on page 63.

INTERPRETATION

The CVI and OBV (On Balance Volume, page 207) are quite similar. Many computer programs and investors incorrectly call the OBV the CVI. OBV, like the CVI, was designed to show if volume is flowing into or out of the market. But, because up-volume and down-volume are not available for individual stocks, OBV assumes that all volume is up-volume when the stock closes higher and that all volume is down-volume when the stock closes lower. The CVI does not have to make this large assumption, because it can use the actual up- and down-volume for the New York Stock Exchange.

One useful method of interpreting the CVI is to look at its overall trend. The CVI shows whether there has been more up-volume or down-volume and how long the current volume trend has been in place. Also, look for divergences (see page 35) that develop between the CVI and a market index. For example, is the market index making a new high while the CVI fails to reach new highs? If so, it is probable that the market will correct to confirm the underlying story told by the CVI.

For additional information on interpreting the CVI, refer to the discussion on OBV (page 207).

EXAMPLE

I wrote the following discussion on the CVI in a software manual in July 18, 1984.

"The trendline on the chart below shows that up-volume exceeded down-volume (on average) for all of 1983. When this rising trend was broken (in February of 1984), the market's weakness was confirmed.

"Since breaking down through its rising trendline, the CVI has begun to trend upward (and sideways) once again. While the market has been down, up-volume has exceeded or equaled down-volume (the CVI is trending upward again). There are two different ways to interpret this: Some investors feel that because the market has failed to go up (even though up-volume has exceeded, or at least kept pace with, down-volume) that the overhead supply is too great. After all, if the market falls when there is more up-volume than down-volume, what is going to happen when there is more down-volume than up-volume? An opposing school of thought is that the CVI shows what the smart money is doing. Therefore, since money is flowing into the market on the up-side, the NYSE should soon correct the divergence and rise too."

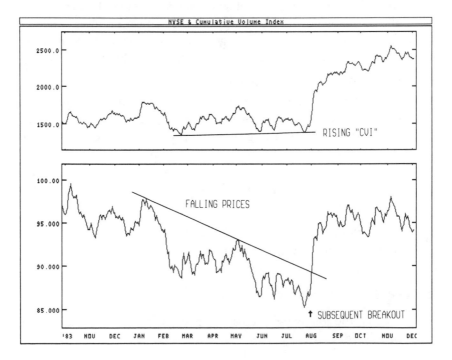

Now that I have the advantage of retrospect, we can see that the CVI was in fact showing "what the smart money" was doing. Shortly after the above commentary was written, the market broke, corrected the divergence, and rose sharply.

CALCULATION

The Cumulative Volume Index is calculated by subtracting the volume of declining stocks from the volume of advancing stocks, and then adding this value to a cumulative total.

CVI = Yesterday's CVI + (Advancing Volume – Declining Volume)

Table 6 shows the calculation of the CVI.

TABLE 6

DATE	ADVANCING	DECLINING	A-D	CVI
02/15/94	175	87	88	88
02/16/94	132	129	3	91
02/17/94	122	183	−61	30
02/18/94	79	171	−92	−62
02/22/94	160	80	80	18

Because the CVI always starts at zero, the numeric value of the CVI is of little importance. What is important is the slope and pattern of the CVI.

Cycles

Overview

Cycles allow us to accurately predict events in nature: bird migrations, the tides, planetary movements, etc. You can also use cycle analysis to predict changes in financial markets, although not always with the accuracy found in nature.

The prices of many commodities reflect seasonal cycles. Due to the agricultural nature of most commodities, these cycles are easily explained and understood. However, for some securities, the cyclical nature is more difficult to explain. Theories as to why certain securities exhibit cyclical patterns range from weather and sunspots, to planetary movement and basic human psychology. I feel human psychology is responsible.

We know that prices are a consensus of human expectations. These expectations are always changing, shifting the supply/demand lines (see page 16), and causing prices to oscillate between overbought and oversold levels. Fluctuations in prices are a natural process of changing expectations and lead to cyclical patterns.

Many technical analysis indicators and tools were developed in an attempt to profit from the cyclical nature of prices. For example, overbought/oversold indicators (e.g., Stochastic Oscillator and Relative Strength Index [RSI]) are designed to help you determine the excessive boundaries of a cycle.

The following illustration shows the major components of a cycle.

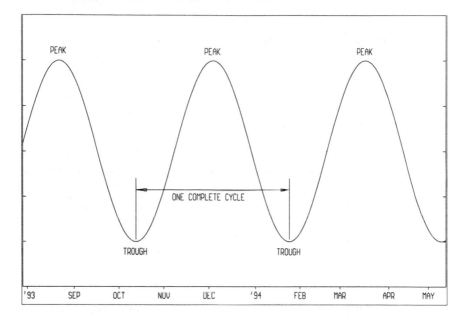

One complete cycle, with peaks and troughs marked across the months from '93 September through May '94.

INTERPRETATION

An entire book could easily be filled with a discussion of cycles and cycle analysis. In the following sections, I briefly explain some of the more popular cycles. A good starting point to learn more about cycles, and technical analysis in general, is Martin Pring's book *Technical Analysis Explained.*

Keep in mind that, in hindsight, you can find patterns in anything. If you are to profit from cycle analysis, the cycle should have a strong track record and it should be used in conjunction with other trading tools.

28-Day Trading Cycle. Research in the 1930s found a 28-day cycle in the wheat market. Some attribute this to the lunar cycle. Regardless of the cause, many markets, including stocks, do appear to have a 28-day cycle. (The 28-day cycle is *calendar* days. This is approximately 20 *trading* days.)

10 1/2-month Futures Cycle. Although individual commodities exhibit their own unique cycles, a cycle ranging between 9 and 12 months has been found in the CRB (Commodity Research Bureau) Index.

January Effect. The stock market has shown an uncanny tendency to end the year higher if prices increase during the month of January, and to end the year with lower prices if prices decline during January. The saying is, "So goes January, so goes the rest of the year." Between 1950 and 1993, the January Effect was correct 38 out of 44 times—an accuracy of 86 percent.

4-Year Cycle (Kitchin Wave). In 1923, Joseph Kitchin found that a 40-month cycle existed in a variety of financial items in both Great Britain and the United States between 1890 and 1922. The four-year cycle was later found to have an extremely strong presence in the stock market between 1868 and 1945.

Although it is called a "four-year cycle," the cycle length has been found to vary between 40 and 53 months.

Presidential Cycle. This cycle is based on the presidential election that occurs every four years in the United States. The concept is that stock prices will decline following the election as the newly elected president takes unpopular steps to make adjustments to the economy. Then at mid-term, stock prices will begin to rise in anticipation of a strong election-day economy.

9.2-Year Cycle (Juglar Wave). In 1860 Clemant Juglar found that a cycle lasting approximately nine years existed in many areas of economic activity. Subsequent research found this cycle to have had a strong presence during the period of 1840 to 1940.

54-Year Cycle (Kondratieff Wave). Named after a Russian economist, the Kondratieff Wave is a long-term, 54-year cycle identified in prices and economic activity. Since the cycle is extremely long-term, it has only repeated itself three times in the stock market.

The up-wave is characterized by rising prices, a growing economy, and mildly bullish stock markets. The plateau is characterized by stable prices, peak economic capacity, and strong bullish stock markets. The down-wave is characterized by falling prices, severe bear markets, and often by a major war.

The following chart of the Kondratieff Wave (from *The Media General Financial Weekly*, June 3, 1974) shows the Kondratieff Wave and U.S. wholesale prices.

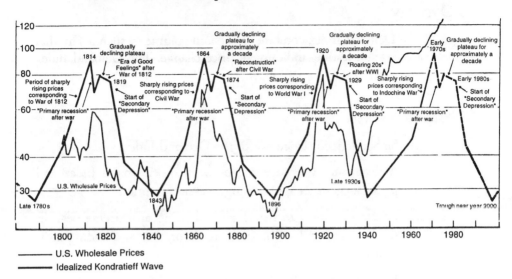

——— U.S. Wholesale Prices

——— Idealized Kondratieff Wave

Demand index

Overview

The Demand Index combines price and volume in such a way that it is often a leading indicator of price change. The Demand Index was developed by James Sibbet.

Interpretation

Mr. Sibbet defined six "rules" for the Demand Index:

1. A divergence (see page 35) between the Demand Index and prices suggests an approaching weakness in price.

2. Prices often rally to new highs following an extreme peak in the Demand Index (the Index is performing as a leading indicator).

3. Higher prices with a lower Demand Index peak usually coincides with an important top (the Index is performing as a coincidental indicator).

4. The Demand Index penetrating the level of zero indicates a change in trend (the Index is performing as a lagging indicator).

5. When the Demand Index stays near the level of zero for any length of time, it usually indicates a weak price movement that will not last long.

6. A large long-term divergence between prices and the Demand Index indicates a major top or bottom.

Example

The following chart shows Procter & Gamble and the Demand Index. A long-term bearish divergence occurred in 1992 as prices rose while the Demand Index fell. According to Sibbet, this indicates a major top.

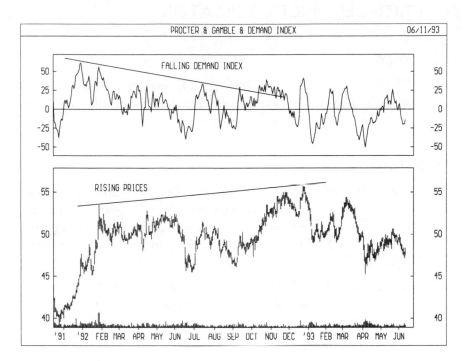

FALLING DEMAND INDEX

RISING PRICES

'91 '92 FEB MAR APR MAY JUN JUL AUG SEP OCT NOV DEC '93 FEB MAR APR MAY JUN

CALCULATION

The Demand Index calculations are too complex for this book (they require 21 columns of data).

Sibbet's original Index plotted the indicator on a scale labeled +0 at the top, 1 in the middle, and –0 at the bottom. Most computer software makes a minor modification to the indicator so that it can be scaled on a normal scale.

Detrended Price Oscillator

Overview

The Detrended Price Oscillator (DPO) attempts to eliminate the trend in prices. Detrended prices allow you to identify cycles and overbought/oversold levels more easily.

Interpretation

Long-term cycles are made up of a series of short-term cycles. Analyzing these shorter-term components of the long-term cycles can be helpful in identifying major turning points in the longer-term cycle. The DPO helps you remove these longer-term cycles from prices.

To calculate the DPO, you specify a time period. Cycles longer than this time period are removed from prices, leaving the shorter-term cycles.

Example

The following chart shows the 20-day DPO of Ryder. You can see that minor peaks in the DPO coincided with minor peaks in Ryder's price, but the longer-term price trend during June was not reflected in the DPO. This is because the 20-day DPO removes cycles of more than 20 days.

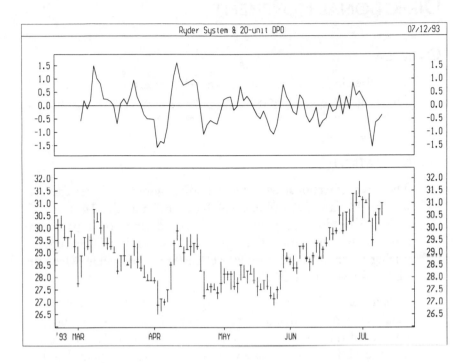

CALCULATION

To calculate the Detrended Price Oscillator, first create an n-period simple moving average (where "n" is the number of periods in the moving average).

$$Moving\ Average = \frac{\sum\limits_{j=1}^{n} Close_j}{n}$$

Now subtract the moving average "(n / 2) + 1" days ago, from the closing price. The result is the DPO.

$DPO = Close - (Moving\ Average\ "((n / 2) + 1)"\ days\ ago)$

DIRECTIONAL MOVEMENT

OVERVIEW

The Directional Movement system helps determine if a security is "trending." It was developed by Welles Wilder and is explained in his book *New Concepts in Technical Trading Systems.*

INTERPRETATION

The basic Directional Movement trading system involves comparing the 14-day +DI (Directional Indicator) and the 14-day –DI. This can be done by plotting the two indicators on top of each other or by subtracting the +DI from the –DI. Wilder suggests buying when the +DI rises above the –DI and selling when the +DI falls below the –DI.

Wilder qualifies these simple trading rules with the "extreme point rule." This rule is designed to prevent whipsaws and reduce the number of trades. The extreme point rule requires that on the day that the +DI and –DI cross, you note the "extreme point." When the +DI rises above the –DI, the extreme price is the high price on the day the lines cross. When the +DI falls below the –DI, the extreme price is the low price on the day the lines cross.

The extreme point is then used as a trigger point at which you should implement the trade. For example, after receiving a buy signal (the +DI rose above the –DI), you should then wait until the security's price rises above the extreme point (the high price on the day that the +DI and –DI lines crossed) before buying. If the price fails to rise above the extreme point, you should continue to hold your short position.

In Wilder's book, he notes that this system works best on securities that have a high Commodity Selection Index (see page 98). He says, "As a rule of thumb, the system will be profitable on commodities that have a CSI value above 25. When the CSI drops below 20, then do not use a trend-following system."

EXAMPLE

The following chart shows Texaco and the +DI and –DI indicators. I drew "buy" arrows when the +DI rose above the –DI and "sell" arrows when the +DI fell below the –DI. I only labeled the significant crossings and did not label the many short-term crossings.

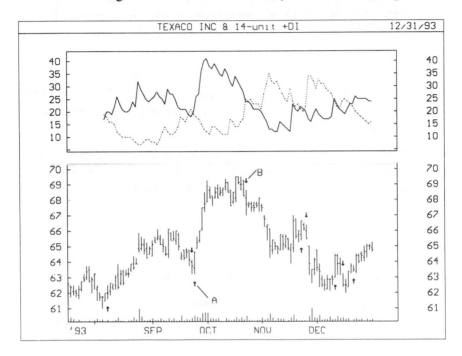

CALCULATION

The calculations of the Directional Movement system are beyond the scope of this book. Wilder's book, *New Concepts In Technical Trading*, gives complete step-by-step instructions on the calculation and interpretation of these indicators.

DOW THEORY

OVERVIEW

In 1897, Charles Dow developed two broad market averages. The Industrial Average included 12 blue-chip stocks and the Rail Average was comprised of 20 railroad enterprises. These are now known as the Dow Jones Industrial Average and the Dow Jones Transportation Average.

The Dow Theory resulted from a series of articles published by Charles Dow in *The Wall Street Journal* between 1900 and 1902. The Dow Theory is the common ancestor to most principles of modern technical analysis.

Interestingly, the theory itself originally focused on using general stock market trends as a barometer for general business conditions. It was not originally intended to forecast stock prices. However, subsequent work has focused almost exclusively on this use of the theory.

INTERPRETATION

The Dow Theory comprises six assumptions:

1. **The Averages Discount Everything.**
    An individual stock's price reflects everything that is known about the security. As new information arrives, market participants quickly disseminate the information and the price adjusts accordingly. Likewise, the market averages discount and reflect everything known by all stock market participants.

2. **The Market Is Comprised of Three Trends.**
    At any given time in the stock market, three forces are in effect: the Primary trend, Secondary trends, and Minor trends.

    The Primary trend can either be a bullish (rising) market or a bearish (falling) market. The Primary trend usually lasts more than one year and may last for several years. If the market is making successive higher-highs and higher-lows the primary trend is up. If the market is making successive lower-highs and lower-lows, the primary trend is down.

Secondary trends are intermediate, corrective reactions to the Primary trend. These reactions typically last from one to three months and retrace from one-third to two-thirds of the previous Secondary trend. The following chart shows a Primary trend (Line A) and two Secondary trends (B and C).

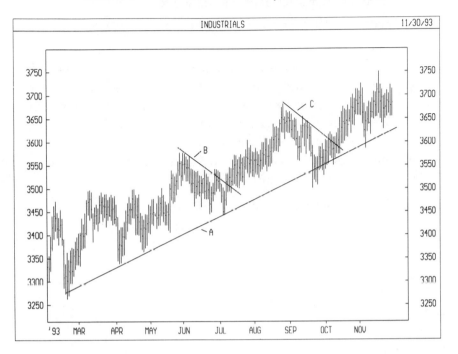

Minor trends are short-term movements lasting from one day to three weeks. Secondary trends are typically comprised of a number of Minor trends. The Dow Theory holds that, since stock prices over the short term are subject to some degree of manipulation (Primary and Secondary trends are not), Minor trends are unimportant and can be misleading.

3. **Primary Trends Have Three Phases.**
   The Dow Theory says that the first phase is made up of aggressive buying by informed investors in anticipation of economic recovery and long-term growth. The general feeling among most investors during this phase is one of "gloom and doom" and "disgust." The informed investors, realizing that a

turnaround is inevitable, aggressively buy from these distressed sellers.

The second phase is characterized by increasing corporate earnings and improved economic conditions. Investors will begin to accumulate stock as conditions improve.

The third phase is characterized by record corporate earnings and peak economic conditions. The general public (having had enough time to forget about their last "scathing") now feels comfortable participating in the stock market—fully convinced that the stock market is headed for the moon. They now buy even more stock, creating a buying frenzy. It is during this phase that those few investors who did the aggressive buying during the first phase begin to liquidate their holdings in anticipation of a downturn.

The following chart of the Dow Industrials illustrates these three phases during the years leading up to the October 1987

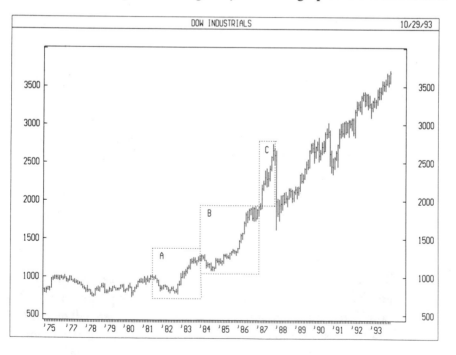

crash. In anticipation of a recovery from the recession, informed investors began to accumulate stock during the first phase (box A). A steady stream of improved earnings reports came in during the second phase (box B), causing more investors to buy stock. Euphoria set in during the third phase (box C), as the general public began to buy stock aggressively.

4. **The Averages Must Confirm Each Other.**
   The Industrials and Transports must confirm each other in order for a valid change of trend to occur. Both averages must extend beyond their previous secondary peak (or trough) in order for a change of trend to be confirmed.

   The following chart shows the Dow Industrials and the Dow Transports at the beginning of the bull market in 1982. Confirmation of the change in trend occurred when both averages rose above their previous secondary peak.

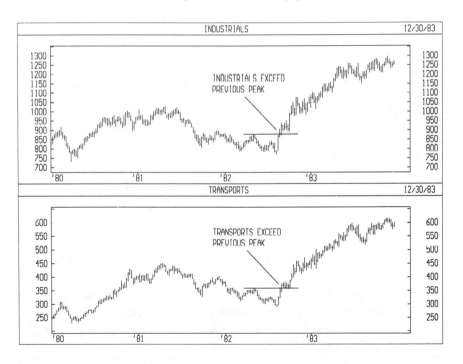

5. **The Volume Confirms the Trend.**
    The Dow Theory focuses primarily on price action. Volume is used only to confirm uncertain situations. Volume should expand in the direction of the primary trend. If the primary trend is down, volume should increase during market declines. If the primary trend is up, volume should increase during market advances.

    The following chart shows expanding volume during an uptrend, confirming the primary trend.

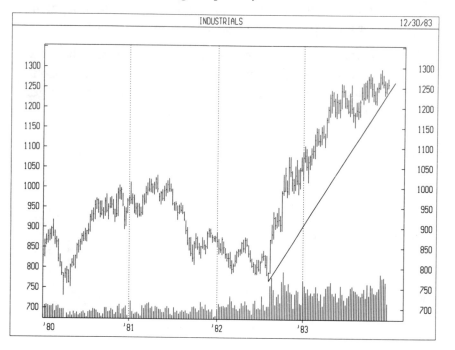

6. **A Trend Remains Intact Until It Gives a Definite Reversal Signal.**
    An uptrend is defined by a series of higher-highs and higher-lows. In order for an uptrend to reverse, prices must have at least one lower high and one lower low (the reverse is true of a downtrend).

    When a reversal in the primary trend is signaled by both the Industrials and Transports, the odds of the new trend continuing are at their greatest. However, the longer a trend continues, the odds of the trend remaining intact become progressively smaller.

The following chart shows how the Dow Industrials registered a higher high (point A) and a higher low (point B), which identified a reversal of the downtrend (line C).

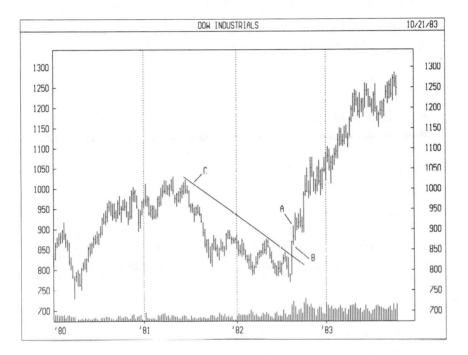

EASE OF MOVEMENT

OVERVIEW

The Ease of Movement indicator shows the relationship between volume and price change. As with Equivolume charting (page 131), this indicator shows how much volume is required to move prices.

The Ease of Movement indicator was developed by Richard W. Arms, Jr., the creator of Equivolume.

INTERPRETATION

High Ease of Movement values occur when prices are moving upward on light volume. Low Ease of Movement values occur when prices are moving downward on light volume. If prices are not moving, or if heavy volume is required to move prices, then the indicator will also be near zero.

The Ease of Movement indicator produces a buy signal when it crosses above zero, indicating that prices are moving upward more easily; a sell signal is given when the indicator crosses below zero, indicating that prices are moving downward more easily.

EXAMPLE

The following chart shows Compaq and a 14-day Ease of Movement indicator. A 9-day moving average was plotted on the Ease of Movement indicator. "Buy" and "sell" arrows were placed on the chart when the moving average crossed zero.

CALCULATION

To calculate the Ease of Movement indicator, first calculate the Midpoint Move as shown below.

$$\left(\frac{Today's\ High\ +\ Today's\ Low}{2} \right) - \left(\frac{Yesterday's\ High\ -\ Yesterday's\ Low}{2} \right)$$

$$Box\ Ratio = \frac{Volume\ (in\ 10,000s\,)}{High - Low}$$

The Ease of Movement (EMV) indicator is then calculated from the Midpoint Move and Box Ratio.

$$EMV = \frac{Midpoint\ Move}{Box\ Ratio}$$

The raw Ease of Movement value is usually smoothed with a moving average.

EFFICIENT MARKET THEORY

OVERVIEW

The Efficient Market Theory says that security prices correctly and almost immediately reflect all information and expectations. It says that you cannot consistently outperform the stock market due to the random nature in which information arrives and the fact that prices react and adjust almost immediately to reflect the latest information. Therefore, it assumes that at any given time, the market correctly prices all securities. The result, or so the theory advocates, is that securities cannot be overpriced or underpriced for a long enough period of time to profit therefrom.

The theory holds that since prices reflect all available information, and since information arrives in a random fashion, there is little to be gained by any type of analysis, whether fundamental or technical. It assumes that every piece of information has been collected and processed by thousands of investors and this information (both old and new) is correctly reflected in the price. Returns cannot be increased by studying historical data, either fundamental or technical, since past data will have no effect on future prices.

The problem with both of these theories is that *many* investors base their expectations on past prices (whether using technical indicators, a strong track record, an oversold condition, industry trends, etc). And since investors' expectations control prices, it seems obvious that past prices do have a significant influence on future prices.

ELLIOTT WAVE THEORY

OVERVIEW

The Elliott Wave Theory is named after Ralph Nelson Elliott. Inspired by the Dow Theory (see page 116) and by observations found throughout nature, Elliott concluded that the movement of the stock market could be predicted by observing and identifying a repetitive pattern of waves. In fact, Elliott believed that all human activities, not just the stock market, were influenced by these identifiable series of waves.

With the help of C. J. Collins, Elliott's ideas received the attention of Wall Street in a series of articles published in *Financial World* magazine in 1939. During the 1950s and 1960s (after Elliott's passing), his work was advanced by Hamilton Bolton. In 1960, Bolton wrote *Elliott Wave Principle—A Critical Appraisal.* This was the first significant work since Elliott's passing. In 1978, Robert Prechter and A. J. Frost collaborated to write the book *Elliott Wave Principle.*

INTERPRETATION

The underlying forces behind the Elliott Wave Theory are of building up and tearing down. The basic concepts of the Elliott Wave Theory are listed below.

1. Action is followed by reaction.

2. There are five waves in the direction of the main trend followed by three corrective waves (a "5-3" move).

3. A 5-3 move completes a cycle. This 5-3 move then becomes two subdivisions of the next higher 5-3 wave.

4. The underlying 5-3 pattern remains constant, though the time span of each may vary.

The basic pattern is made up of eight waves (five up and three down) which are labeled 1, 2, 3, 4, 5, a, b, and c on the following chart.

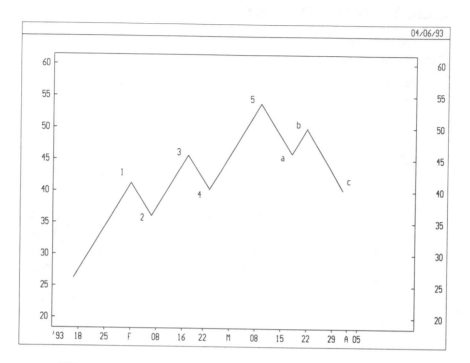

Waves 1, 3, and 5 are called impulse waves. Waves 2 and 4 are called corrective waves. Waves a, b, and c correct the main trend made by waves 1 through 5.

The main trend is established by waves 1 through 5 and can be either up or down. Waves a, b, and c always move in the opposite direction of waves 1 through 5.

Elliott Wave Theory holds that each wave within a wave count contains a complete 5-3 wave count of a smaller cycle. The longest wave count is called the Grand Supercycle. Grand Supercycle waves are comprised of Supercycles, and Supercycles are comprised of Cycles. This process continues into Primary, Intermediate, Minute, Minuette, and Sub-minute waves.

The following chart shows how 5-3 waves are comprised of smaller cycles. This chart contains the identical pattern shown in the preceding chart (now displayed using dotted lines), but the smaller cycles are also displayed. For example, you can see that impulse

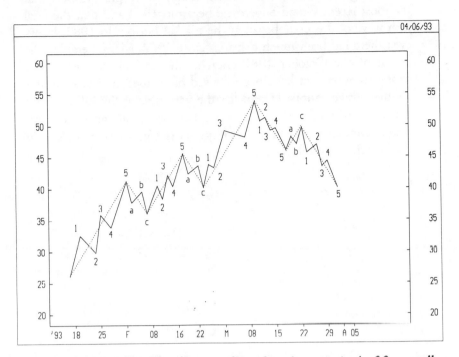

wave labeled "1" in the preceding chart is comprised of five smaller waves.

Fibonacci numbers (see page 134) provide the mathematical foundation for the Elliott Wave Theory. Briefly, the Fibonacci number sequence is made by simply starting at 1 and adding the previous number to arrive at the new number (i.e., 0 + 1 = 1, 1 + 1 = 2, 2 + 1 = 3, 3 + 2 = 5, 5 + 3 = 8, 8 + 5 = 13, etc.). Each of the cycles that Elliott defined is comprised of a total wave count that falls within the Fibonacci number sequence. For example, the preceding chart shows two primary waves (an impulse wave and a corrective wave), eight intermediate waves (the 5-3 sequence shown in the first chart), and 34 minute waves (as labeled). The numbers 2, 8, and 34 fall within the Fibonacci numbering sequence.

Elliott Wave practitioners use their determination of the wave count in combination with the Fibonacci numbers to predict the time span and magnitude of future market moves ranging from minutes and hours to years and decades.

There is general agreement among Elliott Wave practitioners that the most recent Grand Supercycle began in 1932 and that the final fifth wave of this cycle began at the market bottom in 1982. However, there has been much disparity since 1982. Many heralded the arrival of the October 1987 crash as the end of the cycle. The strong recovery that has since followed has caused them to reevaluate their wave counts. Herein lies the weakness of the Elliott Wave Theory—its predictive value is dependent on an accurate wave count. Determining where one wave starts and another wave ends can be extremely subjective.

Envelopes (Trading Bands)

Overview

An envelope is comprised of two moving averages (see page 184). One moving average is shifted upward and the second moving average is shifted downward.

Interpretation

Envelopes define the upper and lower boundaries of a security's normal trading range. A sell signal is generated when the security reaches the upper band, whereas a buy signal is generated at the lower band. The optimum percentage shift depends on the volatility of the security—the more volatile, the larger the percentage.

The logic behind envelopes is that overzealous buyers and sellers push the price to the extremes (i.e., the upper and lower bands), at which point the prices often stabilize by moving to more realistic levels. This is similar to the interpretation of Bollinger Bands (see page 72).

Example

The following chart displays American Brands with a 6 percent envelope of a 25-day exponential moving average. You can see how American Brands' price tended to bounce off the bands rather than penetrate them.

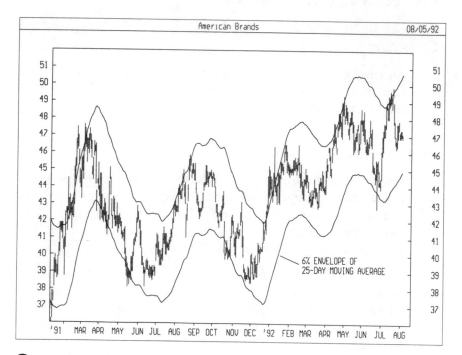

6% ENVELOPE OF
25-DAY MOVING AVERAGE

CALCULATION

Envelopes are calculated by shifted moving averages. In the above example, one 25-day exponential moving average was shifted up 6 percent and another 25-day moving average was shifted down 6 percent.

EQUIVOLUME

OVERVIEW

Equivolume displays prices in a manner that emphasizes the relationship between price and volume. Equivolume was developed by Richard W. Arms, Jr., and is further explained in his book *Volume Cycles in the Stock Market.*

Instead of displaying volume as an "afterthought" on the lower margin of a chart, Equivolume combines price and volume in a two-dimensional box. The top line of the box is the high for the period and the bottom line is the low for the period. The width of the box is the unique feature of Equivolume—it represents the volume for the period.

Figure 46 shows the components of an Equivolume box:

FIGURE 46

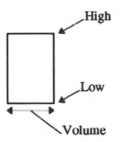

The bottom scale on an Equivolume chart is based on volume, rather than on dates. This suggests that volume, rather than time, is the guiding influence of price change. To quote Mr. Arms, "If the market wore a wristwatch, it would be divided into shares, not hours."

CANDLEVOLUME

Candlevolume charts are a unique hybrid of Equivolume and candlestick charts. Candlevolume charts possess the shadows and body characteristics of candlestick charts (see page 79), plus the volume width attribute of Equivolume charts. This combination gives you the unique ability to study candlestick patterns in combination with their volume-related movements.

INTERPRETATION

The shape of each Equivolume box provides a picture of the supply and demand for the security during a specific trading period. Short and wide boxes (heavy volume accompanied with small changes in price) tend to occur at turning points, while tall and narrow boxes (light volume accompanied with large changes in price) are more likely to occur in established trends.

Especially important are boxes that penetrate support or resistance levels, since volume confirms penetrations (see page 17). A "power box" is one in which both height and width increase substantially. Power boxes provide excellent confirmation of a breakout. A narrow box, due to light volume, puts the validity of a breakout in question.

EXAMPLE

The following Equivolume chart shows Phillip Morris' prices. Note the price consolidation from June to September with resistance

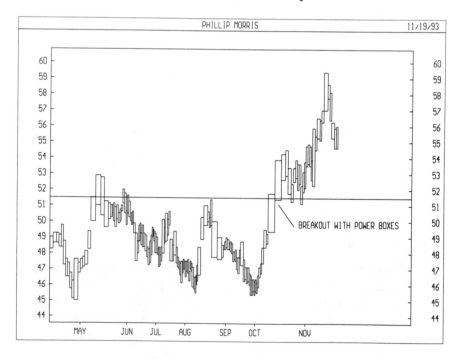

around $51.50. The strong move above $51.50 in October produced a power box validating the breakout.

The following is a Candlevolume chart of the British pound. You can see that this hybrid chart is similar to a candlestick chart (see page 79), but the width of the bars varies based on volume.

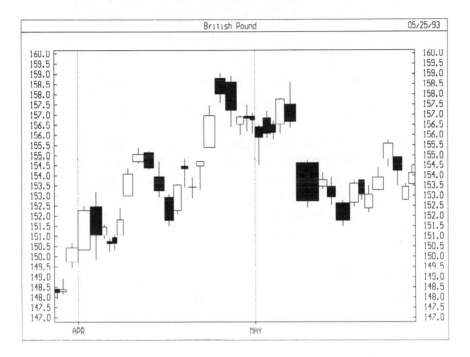

FIBONACCI STUDIES

OVERVIEW

Leonardo Fibonacci was a mathematician who was born in Italy around the year 1170. It is believed that Mr. Fibonacci discovered the relationship of what are now referred to as Fibonacci numbers while studying the Great Pyramid of Gizeh in Egypt.

Fibonacci numbers are a sequence of numbers in which each successive number is the sum of the two previous numbers:

1, 1, 2, 3, 5, 8, 13, 21, 34, 55, 89, 144, 610, etc.

These numbers possess an intriguing number of interrelationships, such as the fact that any given number is approximately 1.618 times the preceding number and any given number is approximately 0.618 times the following number. The booklet *Understanding Fibonacci Numbers* by Edward Dobson contains a good discussion of these interrelationships.

INTERPRETATION

There are four popular Fibonacci studies: arcs, fans, retracements, and time zones. The interpretation of these studies involves anticipating changes in trends as prices near the lines created by the Fibonacci studies.

ARCS

Fibonacci Arcs are displayed by first drawing a trendline between two extreme points, for example, a trough and opposing peak. Three arcs are then drawn, centered on the second extreme point, so they intersect the trendline at the Fibonacci levels of 38.2 percent, 50.0 percent, and 61.8 percent.

The interpretation of Fibonacci Arcs involves anticipating support and resistance as prices approach the arcs. A common technique is to display both Fibonacci Arcs and Fibonacci Fan Lines and to anticipate support/resistance at the points where the Fibonacci studies cross.

Note that the points where the Arcs cross the price data will vary depending on the scaling of the chart, because the Arcs are drawn so that they are circular relative to the chart paper or computer screen.

The following British pound chart illustrates how the arcs can provide support and resistance (points A, B, and C).

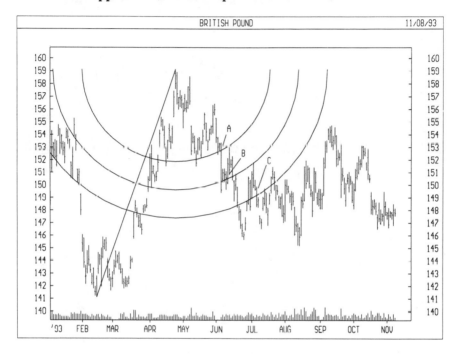

FANS

Fibonacci Fan Lines are displayed by drawing a trendline between two extreme points, for example, a trough and opposing peak. Then an "invisible" vertical line is drawn through the second extreme point. Three trendlines are then drawn from the first extreme point so that they pass through the invisible vertical line at the Fibonacci levels of 38.2 percent, 50.0 percent, and 61.8 percent. (This technique is similar to Speed Resistance Lines, page 260.)

The following chart of Texaco shows how prices found support at the Fan Lines. You can see that when prices encountered the top Fan Line (point A), they were unable to penetrate the line for several days. When prices did penetrate this line, they dropped quickly to the bottom Fan Line (points B and C) before finding support.

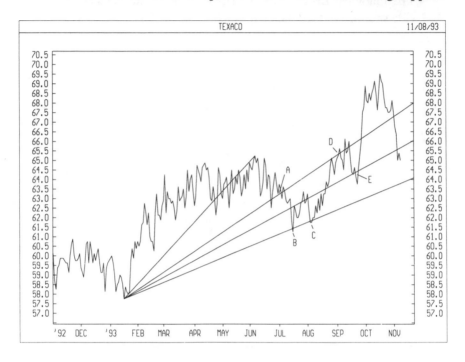

Also note that when prices bounced off the bottom line (point C), they rose freely to the top line (point D), where they again met resistance, fell to the middle line (point E), and rebounded.

RETRACEMENTS

Fibonacci Retracements are displayed by first drawing a trendline between two extreme points, for example, a trough and opposing peak. A series of nine horizontal lines are drawn intersecting the trendline at the Fibonacci levels of 0.0 percent, 23.6 percent, 38.2 percent, 50 percent, 61.8 percent, 100 percent, 161.8 percent,

261.8 percent, and 423.6 percent. (Some of the lines will probably not be visible because they will be off the scale.)

After a significant price move (either up or down), prices will often retrace a significant portion (if not all) of the original move. As prices retrace, support and resistance levels often occur at or near the Fibonacci Retracement levels.

In the following chart of Eastman Kodak, Fibonacci Retracement lines were drawn between a major trough and peak. You can see that support and resistance occurred near the Fibonacci levels of 23 and 38 percent.

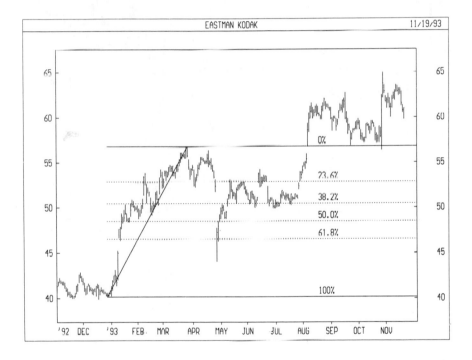

TIME ZONES

Fibonacci Time Zones are a series of vertical lines. They are spaced at the Fibonacci intervals of 1, 2, 3, 5, 8, 13, 21, 34, etc. The interpretation of Fibonacci Time Zones involves looking for significant changes in price near the vertical lines.

In the following example, Fibonacci Time Zones were drawn on the Dow Jones Industrials beginning at the market bottom in 1970. You can see that significant changes in the Industrials occurred on or near the Time Zone lines.

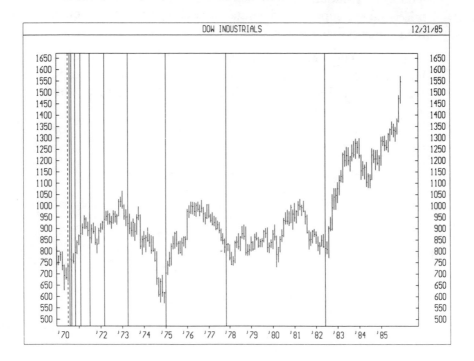

FOUR PERCENT MODEL

OVERVIEW

The Four Percent Model is a stock market timing tool based on the percent change of the weekly close of the (geometric) Value Line Composite Index. It is a trend-following tool designed to keep you in the market during major up moves and out (or short) during major down moves.

The Four Percent Model was developed by Ned Davis and popularized in Martin Zweig's book *Winning on Wall Street.*

INTERPRETATION

A significant strength of the Four Percent Model is its simplicity. The model is easy to calculate and to analyze. In fact, only one piece of data is required—the weekly close of the Value Line Composite Index.

A buy signal is generated when the index rises at least 4 percent from a previous value. A sell signal is generated when the index falls at least 4 percent. For example, a buy signal would be generated if the weekly close of the Value Line rose from 200 to 208 (a 4 percent rise). If the index subsequently rallied to 250 and then dropped below 240 (a 4 percent drop), a sell signal would be generated.

From 1961 to 1992, a buy-and-hold approach on the Value Line Index would have yielded 149 points (3 percent annual return). Using the Four Percent Model (including shorts) during the same period would have yielded 584 points (13.6 percent annual return). Interestingly, about half of the signals generated were wrong. However, the average gain was much larger than the average loss—an excellent example of the stock market maxim "cut your losses short and let your profits run."

EXAMPLE

The following chart shows the Zig Zag indicator (see page 318) plotted on top of the Value Line Composite Index. The Zig Zag indicator identifies changes in price that are at least 4 percent.

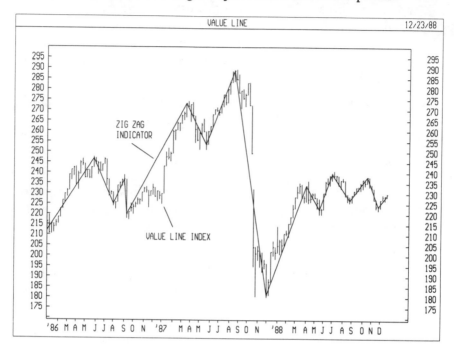

FOURIER TRANSFORM

OVERVIEW

Fourier Transforms were originally developed as an engineering tool to study repetitious phenomena such as the vibration of a stringed musical instrument or an airplane wing during flight. Fourier analysis is used in technical analysis to detect cyclical patterns within prices.

It is beyond the scope of this book to provide a full explanation of Fourier analysis. Further information can be found in *Technical Analysis of Stocks and Commodities* (TASC), Vol. 1, Nos. 2, 4, and 7; Vol. 2, No. 4; Vol. 3, Nos. 2 and 7 ("Understanding Cycles"); Vol. 4, No. 6; Vol. 5, Nos. 3 ("In Search of the Cause of Cycles") and 5 ("Cycles and Chart Patterns"); and Vol. 6, No. 11 ("Cycles").

The complete Fourier analysis concept is called spectral analysis. Fast Fourier Transform (FFT) is an abbreviated calculation that can be computed in a fraction of the time. FFT sacrifices phase relationships and concentrates only on cycle length and amplitude.

The benefit of FFT is its ability to extract the predominate cycle(s) from a series of data (e.g., an indicator or a security's price).

FFTs are based on the principle that any finite, time-ordered set of data can be approximated by decomposing the data into a set of sine waves. Each sine wave has a specific cycle length, amplitude, and phase relationship to the other sine waves.

A difficulty occurs when applying FFT analysis to security prices, because FFTs were designed to be applied to nontrending, periodic data. The fact that security prices are often trending is overcome by "detrending" the data, using either a linear regression trendline or a moving average. To adjust for the fact that security data is not truly periodic, since securities are not traded on weekends and some holidays, the prices are passed through a smoothing function called a "hamming window."

INTERPRETATION

As stated above, it is beyond the scope of this book to provide complete interpretation of FFT analysis. I will focus my discussion on the "Interpreted" Fast Fourier Transforms found in the Meta-Stock computer program. This indicator shows the three predominate cycle lengths and the relative strength of each of these cycles.

The following chart displays the Interpreted FFT of US Steel. The Interpreted FFT shows that predominate cycle lengths in US Steel are 205, 39, and 27 trading days.

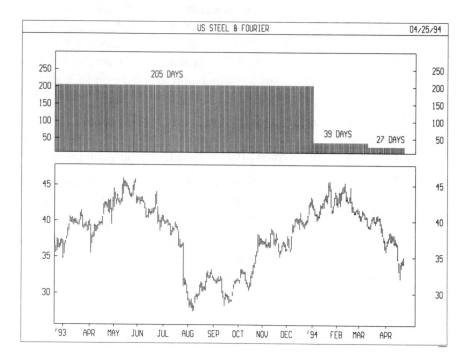

The Interpreted FFT indicator always displays the most significant cycle (205 days in this example) on the left and the least significant cycle (27 days in this example) on the right. The length of each cycle is determined by the numeric value of the indicator (as read from the y-axis scales on the sides of the chart).

The longer the indicator remains at a specific value, the more predominate it was in the data being analyzed. For example, in the above chart, the 205-day cycle is five times stronger than the 39-day cycle, because the indicator was at 205 for a much longer period (the fact that 205 is five times greater than 39 is coincidental).

Once you know the predominate cycle length, you can use it as a parameter for other indicators. In this example, since US Steel has a predominate cycle of 205 days, you may want to plot a 102-day moving average or a 102-day RSI on the security.

FUNDAMENTAL ANALYSIS

OVERVIEW

Fundamental analysis is the study of economic, industry, and company conditions in an effort to determine the value of a company's stock. Fundamental analysis typically focuses on key statistics in a company's financial statements to determine if the stock price is correctly valued.

I realize that some people will find a discussion on *fundamental* analysis within a book on *technical* analysis peculiar, but the two theories are not as different as many people believe. It is quite popular to apply technical analysis to charts of fundamental data, for example, to compare trends in interest rates with changes in security prices. It is also popular to use fundamental analysis to select securities and then use technical analysis to time individual trades. Even diehard technicians can benefit from an understanding of fundamental analysis (and vice versa).

INTERPRETATION

Most fundamental information focuses on economic, industry, and company statistics. The typical approach to analyzing a company involves four basic steps:

1. Determine the condition of the general economy.

2. Determine the condition of the industry.

3. Determine the condition of the company.

4. Determine the value of the company's stock.

ECONOMIC ANALYSIS

The economy is studied to determine if overall conditions are good for the stock market. Is inflation a concern? Are interest rates likely to rise or fall? Are consumers spending? Is the trade balance favorable? Is the money supply expanding or contracting? These are just some of the questions that the fundamental analyst would ask to determine if economic conditions are right for the stock market.

INDUSTRY ANALYSIS

The company's industry obviously influences the outlook for the company. Even the best stocks can post mediocre returns if they are in an industry that is struggling. It is often said that a weak stock in a strong industry is preferable to a strong stock in a weak industry.

COMPANY ANALYSIS

After determining the economic and industry conditions, the company itself is analyzed to determine its financial health. This is usually done by studying the company's financial statements. From these statements a number of useful ratios can be calculated. The ratios fall under five main categories: profitability, price, liquidity, leverage, and efficiency. When performing ratio analysis on a company, the ratios should be compared to other companies within the same or similar industry to get a feel for what is considered "normal." At least one popular ratio from each category is shown below.

Net Profit Margin. A company's net profit margin is a profitability ratio calculated by dividing net income by total sales. This ratio indicates how much profit the company is able to squeeze out of each dollar of sales. For example, a net profit margin of 30 percent indicates that $0.30 of every $1.00 in sales is realized in profits.

P/E Ratio. The P/E ratio (i.e., Price/Earnings ratio) is a price ratio calculated by dividing the security's current stock price by the previous four quarters' earnings per share (EPS).

The P/E Ratio shows how much an investor must pay to "buy" $1 of the company's earnings. For example, if a stock's current price is $20 and the EPS for the last four quarters was $2, the P/E ratio is 10 (i.e., $20 / $2 = 10). This means that you must pay $10 to "buy" $1 of the company's earnings. Of course, investor expectations of company's future performance play a heavy role in determining a company's current P/E ratio.

A common approach is to compare the P/E ratios of companies within the same industry. All else being equal, the company with the lower P/E ratio is the better value.

Book Value Per Share. A company's book value is a price ratio calculated by dividing total net assets (assets minus liabilities) by total shares outstanding. Depending on the accounting methods used and the age of the assets, book value can be helpful in determining if a security is overpriced or underpriced. If a security is selling at a price far below book value, it may be an indication that the security is underpriced.

Current Ratio. A company's current ratio is a liquidity ratio calculated by dividing current assets by current liabilities. This measures the company's ability to meet current debt obligations. The higher the ratio, the more liquid the company. For example, a current ratio of 3.0 means that the company's current assets, if liquidated, would be sufficient to pay for three times the company's current liabilities.

Debt Ratio. A company's debt ratio is a leverage ratio calculated by dividing total liabilities by total assets. This ratio measures the extent to which total assets have been financed with debt. For example, a debt ratio of 40 percent indicates that 40 percent of the company's assets have been financed with borrowed funds. Debt is a two-edged sword. During times of economic stress or rising interest rates, companies with a high debt ratio can experience financial problems. However, during good times, debt can enhance profitability by financing growth at a lower cost.

Inventory Turnover. A company's inventory turnover is an efficiency ratio calculated by dividing cost of goods sold by inventories. It reflects how effectively the company manages its inventories by showing the number of times per year inventories are turned over (replaced). Of course, this type of ratio is highly dependent on the industry. A grocery store chain will have a much higher turnover than a commercial airplane manufacturer. As stated previously, it is important to compare ratios with other companies in the same industry.

STOCK PRICE VALUATION

After determining the condition and outlook of the economy, the industry, and the company, the fundamental analyst is prepared to determine if the company's stock is overvalued, undervalued, or correctly valued.

Several valuation models have been developed to help determine the value of a stock. These include dividend models, which focus on the present value of expected dividends; earnings models, which focus on the present value of expected earnings; and asset models, which focus on the value of the company's assets.

There is no doubt that fundamental factors play a major role in a stock's price. However, if you form your price expectations based on fundamental factors, it is important that you study the price history as well or you may end up owning an undervalued stock that remains undervalued.

GANN ANGLES

OVERVIEW

W. D. Gann (1878–1955) designed several unique techniques for studying price charts. Central to Gann's techniques was geometric angles in conjunction with time and price. Gann believed that specific geometric patterns and angles had unique characteristics that could be used to predict price action.

All of Gann's techniques require that equal time and price intervals be used on the charts, so that a rise/run of 1 × 1 will always equal a 45 degree angle.

INTERPRETATION

Gann believed that the ideal balance between time and price exists when prices rise or fall at a 45 degree angle relative to the time axis. This is also called a 1 × 1 angle (i.e., prices rise one price unit for each time unit).

Gann Angles are drawn between a significant bottom and top (or vice versa) at various angles. Deemed the most important by Gann, the 1 × 1 trendline signifies a bull market if prices are above the trendline or a bear market if below. Gann felt that a 1 × 1 trendline provides major support during an uptrend and when the trendline is broken, it signifies a major reversal in the trend. Gann identified nine significant angles, with the 1 × 1 being the most important:

> 1 × 8 – 82.5 degrees
> 1 × 4 – 75 degrees
> 1 × 3 – 71.25 degrees
> 1 × 2 – 63.75 degrees
> 1 × 1 – 45 degrees
> 2 × 1 – 26.25 degrees
> 3 × 1 – 18.75 degrees
> 4 × 1 – 15 degrees
> 8 × 1 – 7.5 degrees

Note that in order for the rise/run values (e.g., 1 × 1, 1 × 8, etc.) to match the actual angles (in degrees), the x- and y-axes must have equally spaced intervals. This means that one unit on the x-axis (i.e., hour, day, week, month, etc.) must be the same distance as one unit on the y-axis. The easiest way to calibrate the chart is make sure that a 1 × 1 angle produces a 45 degree angle.

Gann observed that each of the angles can provide support and resistance depending on the trend. For example, during an uptrend the 1 × 1 angle tends to provide major support. A major reversal is signaled when prices fall below the 1 × 1 angled trendline. According to Gann, prices should then be expected to fall to the next trendline (i.e., the 2 × 1 angle). In other words, as one angle is penetrated, expect prices to move and consolidate at the next angle.

Gann developed several techniques for studying market action. These include Gann Angles, Gann Fans, Gann Grids, and Cardinal Squares.

EXAMPLES

A Gann Fan displays lines at each of the angles that Gann identified. The following chart shows a Gann Fan on the S&P 500. You can see that the S&P bounced off the 1 × 1 and 2 × 1 lines.

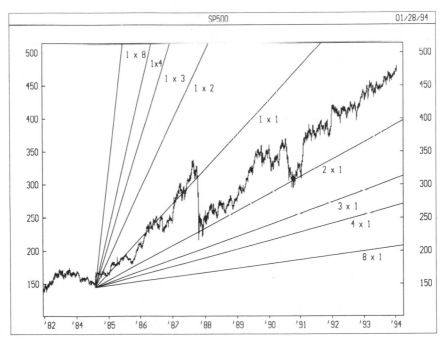

This next chart shows the same S&P 500 data with a Gann Grid. This is an 80 × 80 grid (each line on the grid is 1 × 1 and the lines are spaced 80 weeks apart).

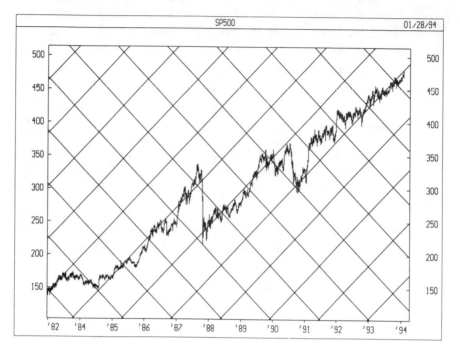

Herrick Payoff Index

Overview

The Herrick Payoff Index (HPI) is designed to show the amount of money flowing into or out of a futures contract. The index uses open interest during its calculations; therefore, the security being analyzed must contain open interest (see page 210).

The Herrick Payoff Index was developed by John Herrick.

Interpretation

When the HPI is above zero, it shows that money is flowing into the futures contract (which is bullish). When the index is below zero, it shows that money is flowing out of the futures contract (which is bearish).

The interpretation of the HPI involves looking for divergences (see page 35) between the index and prices.

Example

The following chart shows the British pound and the HPI. The trendlines identify a bearish divergence where prices were making new highs while the HPI was failing to make new highs. As is typical with divergences, prices corrected to confirm the indicator.

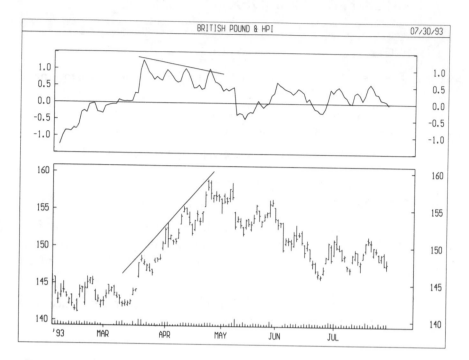

CALCULATION

The HPI requires two inputs, a smoothing factor known as the "multiplying factor" and the "value of a one cent move."

The multiplying factor is part of a smoothing mechanism. The results are similar to the smoothing obtained by a moving average. For example, a multiplying factor of 10 produces results similar to a 10-period moving average.

Mr. Herrick recommends 100 as "the value of a one cent move" for all commodities except silver, which should be 50.

The calculation of the HPI is:

$$\frac{Ky + ((K' - Ky) * S)}{100,000}$$

Where:

Ky = The previous period's HPI

$$K' = (C * V * (M - My)) \left[1 \pm \frac{2 * I}{G} \right]$$

S = The "multiplying factor"

C = The "value of a one cent move"

V = Today's volume

$M = \dfrac{High + Low}{2}$

My = M (mean price) yesterday

$\pm$ = Replace the "$\pm$" symbol with "+" if M is greater than My or with "−" if M is less than My

I = The absolute value of the difference between today's open interest and yesterday's open interest

G = The greater of today's or yesterday's open interest

INTEREST RATES

Interest rates play a key role in the general business cycle and the financial markets. When interest rates change, or interest rate expectations change, the effects are far-reaching. When rates rise, consumers spend less, which causes retail sales to slow, which leads to reduced corporate profits, a declining stock market, and higher unemployment.

The effect of declining corporate profits on the stock market is compounded by the fact that higher interest rates make interest-bearing investments more attractive, causing an exodus of money from the stock market.

INTERPRETATION

Historically, an increase in interest rates is bearish for the stock market, whereas a decrease is bullish.

The following chart shows the four-month rate-of-change of the prime rate and the Dow Industrials. I drew "buy" arrows when interest rates were falling (the indicator was below zero) and "sell" arrows when rates were rising. The arrows show the strong correlation between interest rates and the stock market.

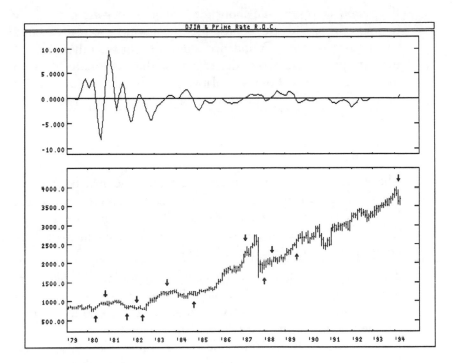

CORPORATE BOND RATES

Just as governments issue bonds to fund their activities, so do corporations. Corporate bonds are considered riskier than Treasury bonds, and they compensate for their higher risk with higher yields. The yield of a specific corporate bond depends on numerous factors. The most important are the financial health of the corporation and prevailing interest rates. Several bond rating services provide investors with an evaluation to help judge the bond's quality.

The Confidence Index, developed by Barron's in 1932, uses corporate bond yields as one of its components. The Confidence Index attempts to measure the "confidence" that investors have in the economy by comparing high-grade bond yields to speculative-grade bond yields.

$$\frac{\textit{Average Yield of High Grade Corporate Bonds}}{\textit{Average Yield of Speculative Grade Corporate Bonds}}$$

If investors are optimistic about the economy, they are more likely to invest in speculative bonds, thereby driving speculative bond yields down, and the Confidence Index up. On the other hand, if they are pessimistic about the economy, they are more likely to move their money from speculative-grade bonds to conservative high-grade bonds, thereby driving high-grade bond yields down and the Confidence Index down.

DISCOUNT RATE

The discount rate is the interest rate that the Federal Reserve charges member banks for loans. Banks use the discount rate as the base for loans made to their customers. The discount rate is set by the Federal Reserve Board, which consists of seven members appointed by the President of the United States.

The discount rate does not fluctuate on a day-to-day basis like most other interest rates. Instead, it only changes when the Federal Reserve Board feels it is necessary to influence the economy. During recessionary times, the Fed will ease interest rates to promote borrowing and spending. During inflationary times, the Fed will raise interest rates to discourage borrowing and spending, thereby slowing the rise in prices.

FEDERAL FUNDS

Banks with excess reserves can lend their reserves to banks with deficient reserves at the Federal Funds Market. The interest rate charged for these short (often just overnight) loans is called the Fed Funds rate.

PRIME RATE

The prime rate is the interest rate U.S. banks charge their best corporate clients. Changes in the prime rate are almost always on the heels of a change in the discount rate.

TREASURY BOND RATES

An extremely important interest rate is the yield on 30-year Treasury bonds ("long bonds"). The U.S. Treasury Department auctions these bonds every six months.

Long bonds are the most volatile of all government bonds, because of the length of their maturities—a small change in interest rates causes an amplified change in the underlying bonds' price.

TREASURY BILL RATES

Treasury bills are short-term (13- and 26-week) money market instruments. They are auctioned by the U.S. Treasury Department weekly and are often used as a secure place to earn current market rates.

EXAMPLE

The following chart shows several interest rates side-by-side.

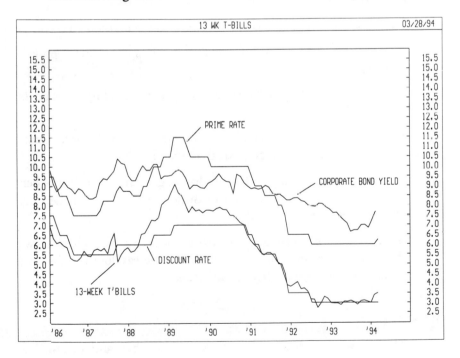

KAGI

OVERVIEW

Kagi charts are believed to have been created around the time that the Japanese stock market began trading in the 1870s. Kagi charts display a series of connecting vertical lines where the thickness and direction of the lines are dependent on the price action. The charts ignore the passage of time.

If prices continue to move in the same direction, the vertical line is extended. However, if prices reverse by a "reversal" amount, a new Kagi line is then drawn in a new column. When prices penetrate a previous high or low, the thickness of the Kagi line changes.

Kagi charts were brought to the United States by Steven Nison when he published the book *Beyond Candlesticks*.

INTERPRETATION

Kagi charts illustrate the forces of supply and demand on a security:

- A series of thick lines shows that demand is exceeding supply (a rally).

- A series of thin lines shows that supply is exceeding demand (a decline).

- Alternating thick and thin lines shows that the market is in a state of equilibrium (i.e., supply equals demand).

The most basic trading technique for Kagi charts is to buy when the Kagi line changes from thin to thick and to sell when the Kagi line changes from thick to thin.

A sequence of higher-highs and higher-lows on a Kagi chart shows that the underlying forces are bullish, whereas lower-highs and lower-lows indicate underlying weakness.

EXAMPLE

The following chart shows a 0.02-point Kagi chart and a classic bar chart of Eurodollars. I drew "buy" arrows on the bar chart when the Kagi lines changed from thin to thick and drew "sell" arrows when the lines changed from thick to thin.

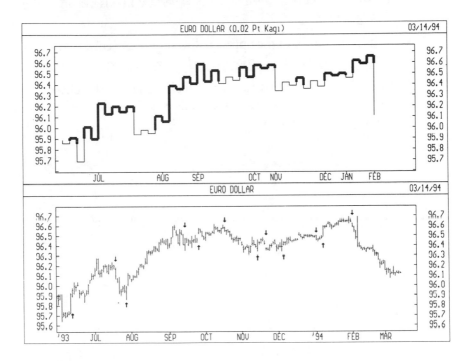

CALCULATION

The first closing price in a Kagi chart is the "starting price." To draw the first Kagi line, today's close is compared to the starting price.

- If today's price is greater than or equal to the starting price, then a thick line is drawn from the starting price to the new closing price.

- If today's price is less than or equal to the starting price, then a thin line is drawn from the starting price to the new closing price.

To draw subsequent lines, compare the closing price to the tip (i.e. bottom or top) of the previous Kagi line:

- If the price continues in the same direction as the previous line, the line is extended in the same direction, no matter how small the move.

- If the price moves in the opposite direction by at least the reversal amount (this may take several days), then a short horizontal line is drawn to the next column and a new vertical line is drawn to the closing price.

- If the price moves in the opposite direction to the current column by less than the reversal amount, no lines are drawn.

If a thin Kagi line exceeds the prior high point on the chart, the line becomes thick. Likewise, if a thick Kagi line falls below the prior low point, the line becomes thin.

LARGE BLOCK RATIO

OVERVIEW

This market sentiment indicator shows the relationship between large block trades, which are trades of more than 10,000 shares, and the total volume on the New York Stock Exchange. The comparison of large block trades to total volume shows how active the large institutional traders are.

The higher the Large Block Ratio, the more institutional activity is taking place. To smooth out the day-to-day fluctuations, I recommend plotting a 20-day moving average of the Large Block Ratio.

INTERPRETATION

A high number of Large Block trades in relation to total volume often coincides with market tops and bottoms. This occurs as institutions recognize the extreme overbought or oversold conditions of the market and place trades accordingly. Of course, this assumes the institutions know what they are doing!

EXAMPLE

The following chart shows the New York Stock Exchange Index and the Large Block Ratio. I drew vertical lines when the Ratio was relatively high. You can see that these points coincided with intermediate-term peaks.

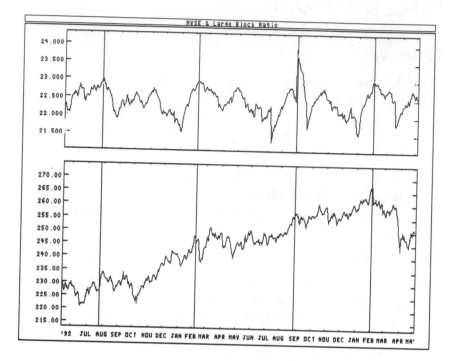

NVSE & Large Block Ratio

CALCULATION

The Large Block Ratio is calculated by dividing the number of large block trades by the total volume on the New York Stock Exchange.

$$\frac{Number\ of\ Large\ Blocks}{Total\ NYSE\ Volume}$$

LINEAR REGRESSION LINES

OVERVIEW

Linear regression is a statistical tool used to predict future values from past values. In the case of security prices, it is commonly used to determine when prices are overextended.

A Linear Regression trendline uses the least squares method to plot a straight line through prices so as to minimize the distances between the prices and the resulting trendline.

INTERPRETATION

If you had to guess what a particular security's price would be tomorrow, a logical guess would be "fairly close to today's price." If prices are trending up, a better guess might be "fairly close to today's price with an upward bias." Linear regression analysis is the statistical confirmation of these logical assumptions.

A Linear Regression trendline is simply a trendline drawn between two points using the least squares fit method. The trendline is displayed in the exact middle of the prices. If you think of this trendline as the "equilibrium" price, any move above or below the trendline indicates overzealous buyers or sellers.

A popular method of using the Linear Regression trendline is to construct Raff Regression Channel lines. Developed by Gilbert Raff, the channel is constructed by plotting two parallel, equidistant lines above and below a Linear Regression trendline. The distance between the channel lines and the regression line is the greatest distance that any one high or low price is from the regression line. Regression Channels contain price movement, with the bottom channel line providing support and the top channel line providing resistance. Prices may extend outside the channel for a short period of time. However, if prices remain outside the channel for a longer period of time, a reversal in trend may be imminent.

A Linear Regression trendline shows where equilibrium exists. Raff Regression Channels show the range in which prices can be expected to deviate from a Linear Regression trendline.

The Time Series Forecast indicator (see page 278) displays the same information as a Linear Regression trendline. Any point along the Time Series Forecast is equal to the ending value of a Linear Regression trendline. For example, the ending value of a Linear Regression trendline that covers 10 days will have the same value as a 10-day Time Series Forecast.

EXAMPLE

The following chart shows the Japanese yen with a Raff Regression Channel.

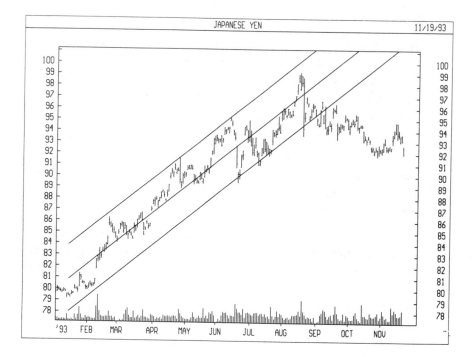

CALCULATION

The linear regression formula is:

$y = a + bx$

Where:

$$a = \frac{\sum y - b \sum x}{n}$$

$$b = \frac{n \sum (xy) - (\sum x)(\sum y)}{n \sum x^2 - (\sum x)^2}$$

x = The current time period

n = The total number of time periods

MACD

The MACD (Moving Average Convergence/Divergence) is a trend-following momentum indicator that shows the relationship between two moving averages of prices. The MACD was developed by Gerald Appel, publisher of *Systems and Forecasts*.

The MACD is the difference between a 26-day and 12-day exponential moving average. A 9-day exponential moving average, called the "signal" (or "trigger") line, is plotted on top of the MACD to show buy/sell opportunities. (Appel specifies exponential moving averages as percentages, as explained on page 188. Thus, he refers to these three moving averages as 7.5 percent, 15 percent, and 20 percent, respectively.)

INTERPRETATION

The MACD proves most effective in wide-swinging trading markets. There are three popular ways to use the MACD: crossovers, overbought/oversold conditions, and divergences.

CROSSOVERS

The basic MACD trading rule is to sell when the MACD falls below its signal line. Similarly, a buy signal occurs when the MACD rises above its signal line. It is also popular to buy/sell when the MACD goes above/below zero.

OVERBOUGHT/OVERSOLD CONDITIONS

The MACD is also useful as an overbought/oversold indicator. When the shorter moving average pulls away dramatically from the longer moving average (i.e., the MACD rises), it is likely that the security price is overextending and will soon return to more realistic levels. MACD overbought and oversold conditions vary from security to security.

An indication that an end to the current trend may be near occurs when the MACD diverges from the security (see page 35). A bearish divergence occurs when the MACD is making new lows while prices fail to reach new lows. A bullish divergence occurs when the MACD is making new highs while prices fail to reach new highs. Both of these divergences are most significant when they occur at relatively overbought/oversold levels.

EXAMPLE

The following chart shows Whirlpool and its MACD. I drew "buy" arrows when the MACD rose above its signal line and drew "sell" arrows when the MACD fell below its signal line.

This chart shows that the MACD is truly a trend-following indicator—sacrificing early signals in exchange for keeping you on the right side of the market. When a significant trend developed, such as in October 1993 and beginning in February 1994, the MACD was able to capture the majority of the move. When the trend was short-lived, such as in January 1993, the MACD proved unprofitable.

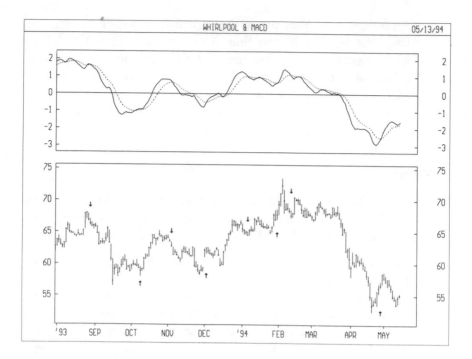

CALCULATION

The MACD is calculated by subtracting the value of a 26-day exponential moving average from a 12-day exponential moving average. A 9-day dotted exponential moving average of the MACD (the "signal" line) is then plotted on top of the MACD.

Mass index

Overview

The Mass Index was designed to identify trend reversals by measuring the narrowing and widening of the range between the high and low prices. As this range widens, the Mass Index increases; as the range narrows, the Mass Index decreases.

The Mass Index was developed by Donald Dorsey.

Interpretation

According to Mr. Dorsey, the most significant pattern to watch for is a "reversal bulge." A reversal bulge occurs when a 25-period Mass Index rises above 27.0 and subsequently falls below 26.5. A reversal in price is then likely. The overall price trend (i.e., trending or trading range) is unimportant.

A nine-period exponential moving average of prices is often used to determine whether the reversal bulge indicates a buy or sell signal. When the reversal bulge occurs, you should buy if the moving average is trending down (in anticipation of the reversal) and sell if it is trending up.

Example

The following chart shows Litton and its Mass Index. A nine-day exponential moving average is plotted on top of Litton's prices. I drew arrows when a reversal bulge occurred (i.e., the Mass Index rose above 27 and then fell below 26.5). If the nine-day moving average was falling, I drew a "buy" arrow. If the nine-day moving average was rising, I drew a "sell" arrow.

You can see that the signals generated by the Mass Index during this time period occurred a few days before the trend reversed.

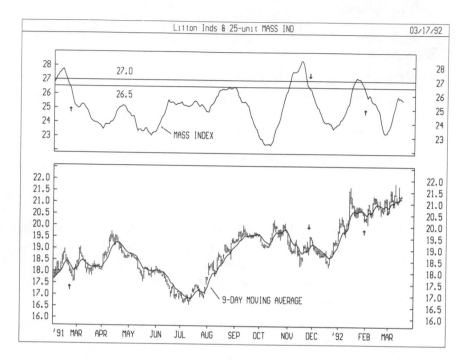

CALCULATION

To calculate the Mass Index:

1. Calculate a nine-day exponential moving average (EMA) of the difference between the high and low prices.

2. Calculate a nine-day exponential moving average of the moving average calculated in Step 1.

3. Divide the moving average calculated in Step 1 by the moving average calculated in Step 2.

4. Total the values in Step 3 for the number of periods in the Mass Index (e.g., 25 days).

$$\sum_{1}^{25}\left[\frac{9\text{--}day\ EMA\ of\ (High-Low)}{9\text{--}day\ EMA\ of\ a\ 9\text{--}day\ EMA\ of\ (High-Low)}\right]$$

MCCLELLAN OSCILLATOR

OVERVIEW

The McClellan Oscillator is a market breadth indicator that is based on the smoothed difference between the number of advancing and declining issues on the New York Stock Exchange.

The McClellan Oscillator was developed by Sherman and Marian McClellan. Extensive coverage of the Oscillator is provided in their book *Patterns for Profit.*

INTERPRETATION

Indicators that use advancing and declining issues to determine the amount of participation in the movement of the stock market are called "breadth" indicators. A healthy bull market is accompanied by a large number of stocks making moderate upward advances in price. A weakening bull market is characterized by a small number of stocks making large advances in price, giving the false appearance that all is well. This type of divergence often signals an end to the bull market. A similar interpretation applies to market bottoms, where the market index continues to decline while fewer stocks are declining.

The McClellan Oscillator is one of the most popular breadth indicators (another popular breadth indicator is the Advance/Decline Line, page 56). Buy signals are typically generated when the McClellan Oscillator falls into the oversold area of −70 to −100 and then turns up. Sell signals are generated when the oscillator rises into the overbought area of +70 to +100 and then turns down.

If the oscillator goes *beyond* these areas (i.e., rises above +100 or falls below −100), it is a sign of an extremely overbought or oversold condition. These extreme readings are usually a sign of a continuation of the current trend.

For example, if the oscillator falls to −90 and turns up, a buy signal is generated. However, if the Oscillator falls below −100, the market will probably trend lower during the next two or three weeks.

You should postpone buying until the Oscillator makes a series of rising bottoms or the market regains strength.

Example

The following chart illustrates the five "trading zones" of the McClellan Oscillator (i.e., above +100, between +70 and +100, between +70 and –70, between –70 and –100, and below –100).

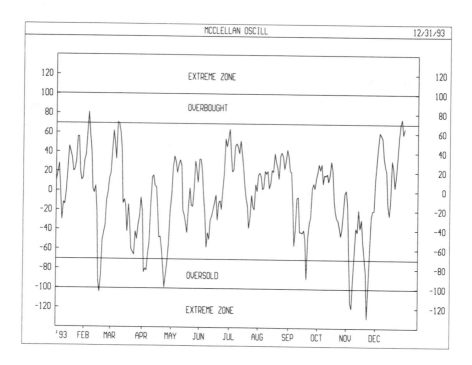

This next chart shows the McClellan Oscillator and the Dow Industrials. I drew "buy" arrows when the Oscillator rose above –70 and "sell" arrows when the Oscillator fell below +70. This indicator does an *excellent* job of timing entry and exit points.

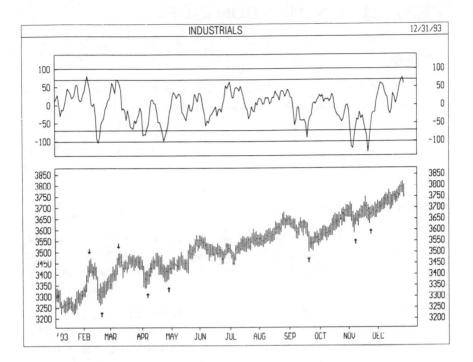

INDUSTRIALS   12/31/93

CALCULATION

The McClellan Oscillator is the difference between 10 percent (approximately 19-day) and 5 percent (approximately 39-day) exponential moving averages of advancing minus declining issues.

(10% EMA of Advances-Declines) – (5% EMA of Advances-Declines)

McClellan Summation Index

Overview

The McClellan Summation Index is a market breadth indicator based on the McClellan Oscillator (see page 171).

The McClellan Summation Index was developed by Sherman and Marian McClellan. Extensive coverage of the index is provided in their book *Patterns for Profit.*

Interpretation

The McClellan Summation Index is a long-term version of the McClellan Oscillator. Its interpretation is similar to that of the McClellan Oscillator except that it is more suited to major trend reversals.

As explained in the Calculation section below, there are two methods to calculate the Summation Index. The two calculation methods create indicators with identical appearances, but their numeric values differ. These interpretational comments refer to the "suggested" calculation method explained in the Calculation section.

McClellan suggests the following rules for use with the Summation Index:

- Look for major bottoms when the Summation Index falls below −1300.

- Look for major tops to occur when a divergence (see page 35) with the market occurs above a Summation Index level of +1600.

- The beginning of a significant bull market is indicated when the Summation Index crosses above +1900 after moving upward more than 3600 points from its prior low (e.g., the index moves from −1600 to +2000).

Example

The following chart shows the McClellan Summation Index and the New York Stock Exchange Index. At the point labeled A, the

Summation Index fell below –1300. This signified a major bottom. The point labeled B indicated the beginning of a significant bull market, because the Summation Index rose above +1900 after moving upward more than 3600 points from its prior low.

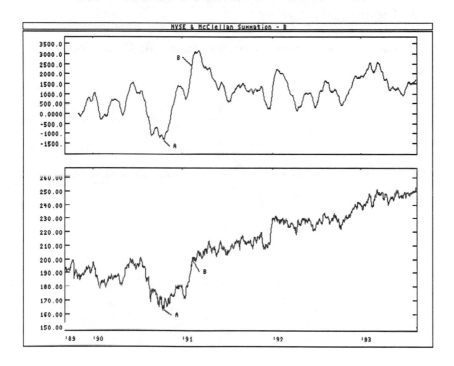

CALCULATION

The McClellan Summation Index can be calculated using two different methods. This first method is the suggested method promoted by Mr. McClellan. It subtracts 10 percent (approximately 19-day) and 5 percent (approximately 39-day) exponential moving averages of advancing minus declining issues from the McClellan Oscillator.

Summation Index = McClellan Oscillator –
((10 * 10% trend) + (20 * 5% trend)) + 1000

Where:

5% trend = 5% EMA of (Advancing – Declining Issues)

10% trend = 10% EMA of (Advancing – Declining Issues)

The second method is to calculate a cumulative sum of the McClellan Oscillator values:

Summation Index = Yesterday's Summation Index + McClellan Oscillator

MEDIAN PRICE

OVERVIEW

The Median Price indicator is simply the midpoint of each day's price. The Typical Price (see page 291) and Weighted Close (see page 312) are similar indicators.

INTERPRETATION

The Median Price indicator provides a simple, single-line chart of the day's "average price." This average price is useful when you want a simpler view of prices.

EXAMPLE

The following chart shows the Median Price indicator (dotted line) on top of Keycorp's bar chart.

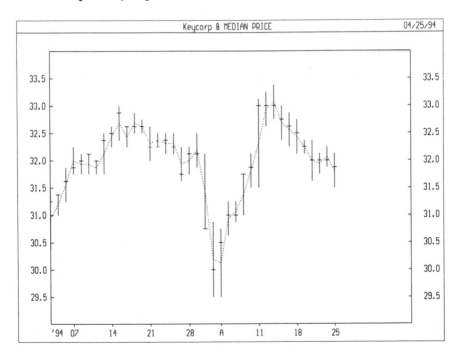

CALCULATION

The Median Price indicator is calculated by adding the high and low price and dividing by two.

$$\frac{High + Low}{2}$$

MEMBER SHORT RATIO

OVERVIEW

The Member Short Ratio (MSR) is a market sentiment indicator that measures the short selling activity of members of the New York Stock Exchange. "Members" trade on the floor of the exchange, either for their own account or for their clients. Stocks are sold short in anticipation of the price falling.

Knowing what the "smart money" is doing (e.g., Members) is often a good indication of the near-term market direction.

The MSR is the inverse of the Public Short Ratio (see page 246). This is because there are only two players in the market, the Public and the Members (Members are further divided into Specialists and Others). When the Public Short Ratio is 20 percent, the Member Short Ratio must be 80 percent.

INTERPRETATION

Because the MSR is the inverse of the PSR, interpretation of the MSR is the opposite of the PSR. When the members are short (a high MSR), you should be short, and when the members are long (a low MSR), you should be long. For more information on interpreting the MSR, refer to the discussion on the Public Short Ratio (see page 246).

CALCULATION

The Member Short Ratio is calculated by dividing the number of member shorts (defined as total short sales minus public short sales) by the total number of short sales. The resulting figure shows the percentage of shorts that were made by members of the New York Stock Exchange.

$$\frac{\textit{Total Short Sales} - \textit{Public Short Sales}}{\textit{Total Short Sales}}$$

MOMENTUM

OVERVIEW

The Momentum indicator measures the amount that a security's price has changed over a given time span.

INTERPRETATION

The interpretation of the Momentum indicator is identical to the interpretation of the Price ROC (see page 243). Both indicators display the rate of change of a security's price. However, the Price ROC indicator displays the rate of change as a percentage, whereas the Momentum indicator displays the rate of change as a ratio.

There are basically two ways to use the Momentum indicator:

- You can use the Momentum indicator as a trend-following oscillator similar to the MACD (this is the method I prefer). Buy when the indicator bottoms and turns up and sell when the indicator peaks and turns down. You may want to plot a short-term (e.g., nine-period) moving average of the indicator to determine when it is bottoming or peaking.

  If the Momentum indicator reaches extremely high or low values (relative to its historical values), you should assume a continuation of the current trend. For example, if the Momentum indicator reaches extremely high values and then turns down, you should assume prices will probably go still higher. In either case, trade only after prices confirm the signal generated by the indicator (e.g., if prices peak and turn down, wait for prices to begin to fall before selling).

- You can also use the Momentum indicator as a leading indicator. This method assumes that market tops are typically identified by a rapid price increase (when everyone expects prices to go higher) and that market bottoms typically end with rapid price declines (when everyone wants to get out). This is often the case, but it is also a broad generalization.

  As a market peaks, the Momentum indicator will climb sharply and then fall off—diverging from the continued upward or sideways movement of the price. Similarly, at a market bottom, Momentum will drop sharply and then begin to climb well ahead of prices. Both of these situations result in divergences (see page 35) between the indicator and prices.

EXAMPLE

The following chart shows Integrated Circuits and its 12-day Momentum indicator. Divergences at points A and B provided leading indications of the reversals that followed.

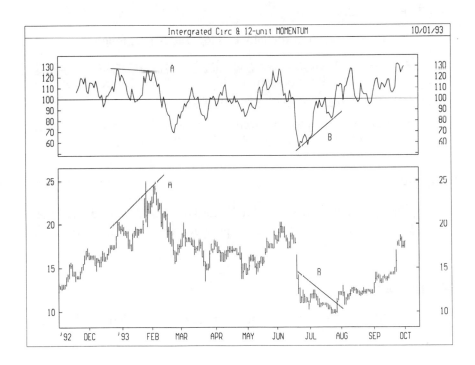

CALCULATION

The Momentum indicator is the ratio of today's price compared to the price x-periods ago.

$$\left(\frac{Close}{Close \ x-time \ periods \ ago} \right) * 100$$

MONEY FLOW INDEX

OVERVIEW

The Money Flow Index (MFI) is a momentum indicator that measures the strength of money flowing in and out of a security. It is related to the Relative Strength Index (RSI, see page 255), but whereas the RSI incorporates only prices, the Money Flow Index accounts for volume.

INTERPRETATION

The interpretation of the Money Flow Index is as follows:

- Look for divergence (see page 35) between the indicator and the price action. If the price trends higher and the MFI trends lower (or vice versa), a reversal may be imminent.

- Look for market tops to occur when the MFI is above 80. Look for market bottoms to occur when the MFI is below 20.

EXAMPLE

The following chart shows Intel and its 14-day Money Flow Index. Divergences at points A and B provided leading indications of the reversals that followed.

CALCULATION

The Money Flow Index requires a series of calculations. First, the period's Typical Price is calculated.

$$Typical\ Price = \frac{High + Low + Close}{3}$$

Next, Money Flow (not the Money Flow Index) is calculated by multiplying the period's Typical Price by the volume.

$$Money\ Flow = Typical\ Price * Volume$$

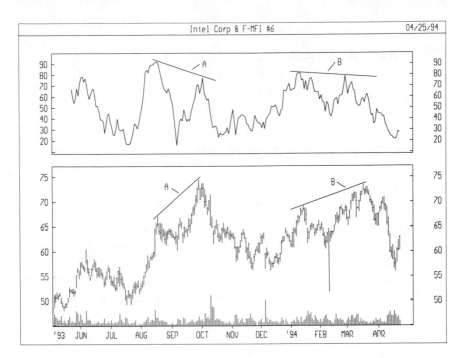

If today's Typical Price is greater than yesterday's Typical Price, it is considered Positive Money Flow. If today's price is less, it is considered Negative Money Flow.

Positive Money Flow is the sum of the Positive Money over the specified number of periods. Negative Money Flow is the sum of the Negative Money over the specified number of periods.

The Money Ratio is then calculated by dividing the Positive Money Flow by the Negative Money Flow.

$$Money\ Ratio = \frac{Positive\ Money\ Flow}{Negative\ Money\ Flow}$$

Finally, the Money Flow Index is calculated using the Money Ratio.

$$Money\ Flow\ Index = 100 - \left[\frac{100}{1 + Money\ Ratio} \right]$$

MOVING AVERAGES

OVERVIEW

A Moving Average is an indicator that shows the average value of a security's price over a period of time. When calculating a moving average, a mathematical analysis of the security's average value over a predetermined time period is made. As the security's price changes, its average price moves up or down.

There are five popular types of moving averages: simple (also referred to as arithmetic), exponential, triangular, variable, and weighted. Moving averages can be calculated on any data series, including a security's open, high, low, close, volume, or another indicator. A moving average of another moving average is also common.

The only significant difference between the various types of moving averages is the weight assigned to the most recent data. Simple moving averages apply equal weight to the prices. Exponential and weighted averages apply more weight to recent prices. Triangular averages apply more weight to prices in the middle of the time period. And variable moving averages change the weighting based on the volatility of prices.

INTERPRETATION

The most popular method of interpreting a moving average is to compare the relationship between a moving average of the security's price with the security's price itself. A buy signal is generated when the security's price rises above its moving average, and a sell signal is generated when the security's price falls below its moving average.

The following chart shows the Dow Jones Industrial Average (DJIA) from 1970 through 1993. Also displayed is a 15-month simple moving average. "Buy" arrows were drawn when the DJIA's close rose above its moving average; "sell" arrows were drawn when it closed below its moving average.

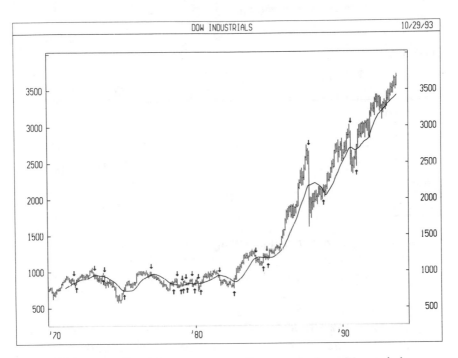

This type of moving average trading system is not intended to get you in at the exact bottom nor out at the exact top. Rather, it is designed to keep you in line with the security's price trend by buying shortly after the security's price bottoms and selling shortly after it tops.

The critical element in a moving average is the number of time periods used in calculating the average. When using hindsight, you can always find a moving average that would have been profitable (using a computer, I found that the optimum number of months in the preceding chart would have been 43). The key is to find a moving average that will be consistently profitable. The most popular moving average is the 39-week (or 200-day) moving average. This moving average has an excellent track record in timing the major (long-term) market cycles.

The length of a moving average should fit the market cycle you wish to follow. [See Table 7.] For example, if you determine that a security has a 40-day peak-to-peak cycle, the ideal moving average length would be 21 days calculated using the following formula:

$$Ideal\ Moving\ Average\ Length = \frac{Cycle\ Length}{2} + 1$$

TABLE 7

TREND	MOVING AVERAGE
Very Short Term	5–13 days
Short Term	14–25 days
Minor Intermediate	26–49 days
Intermediate	50–100 days
Long Term	100–200 days

You can convert a daily moving average quantity into a weekly moving average quantity by dividing the number of days by 5 (e.g., a 200-day moving average is almost identical to a 40-week moving average). To convert a daily moving average quantity into a monthly quantity, divide the number of days by 21 (e.g., a 200-day moving average is very similar to a 9-month moving average, because there are approximately 21 trading days in a month).

Moving averages can also be calculated and plotted on indicators. The interpretation of an indicator's moving average is similar to the interpretation of a security's moving average: When the indicator rises above its moving average, it signifies a continued upward movement by the indicator; when the indicator falls below its moving average, it signifies a continued downward movement by the indicator.

Indicators that are especially well-suited for use with moving average penetration systems include the MACD, Price ROC, Momentum, and Stochastics.

Some indicators, such as short-term Stochastics, fluctuate so erratically that it is difficult to tell what their trend really is. By erasing the indicator and then plotting a moving average of the indicator, you can see the general trend of the indicator rather than its day-to-day fluctuations.

Whipsaws can be reduced, at the expense of slightly later signals, by plotting a short-term moving average (e.g., 2–10 day) of oscillating indicators such as the 12-day ROC, Stochastics, or the RSI. For example, rather than selling when the Stochastic Oscillator falls below 80, you might sell only when a 5-period moving average of the Stochastic Oscillator falls below 80.

EXAMPLE

The following chart shows Lincoln National and its 39-week exponential moving average. Although the moving average does not pinpoint the tops and bottoms perfectly, it does provide a good indication of the direction prices are trending.

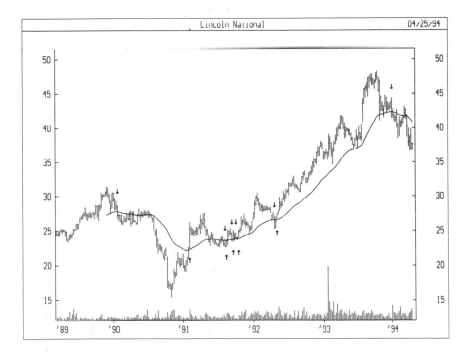

CALCULATION

The following sections explain how to calculate moving averages of a security's price using the various calculation techniques.

SIMPLE

A simple, or arithmetic, moving average is calculated by adding the closing price of the security for a number of time periods (e.g., 12 days) and then dividing this total by the number of time periods. The result is the average price of the security over the time period. Simple moving averages give equal weight to each daily price.

For example, to calculate a 21-day moving average of IBM: First, you would add IBM's closing prices for the most recent 21 days. Next, you would divide that sum by 21; this would give you the average price of IBM over the preceding 21 days. You would plot this average price on the chart. You would perform the same calculation tomorrow: add up the previous 21 days' closing prices, divide by 21, and plot the resulting figure on the chart.

$$\frac{\sum_{1}^{N} closing\ price}{n}$$

Where:

n = The number of time periods in the moving average

EXPONENTIAL

An exponential (or exponentially weighted) moving average is calculated by applying a percentage of today's closing price to yesterday's moving average value. Exponential moving averages place more weight on recent prices.

For example, to calculate a 9 percent exponential moving average of IBM, you would first take today's closing price and multiply it by 9 percent. Next, you would add this product to the value of yesterday's moving average multiplied by 91 percent (100% - 9% = 91%).

*(Today's Close * 0.09) + (Yesterday's Moving Average * 0.91)*

Because most investors feel more comfortable working with time periods rather than with percentages, the exponential percentage can be converted into an approximate number of days. For example, a 9 percent moving average is equal to a 21.2-time-period (rounded to 21) exponential moving average.

The formula for converting exponential percentages to time periods is:

$$Time\ Periods = \left(\frac{2}{Percentage}\right) - 1$$

You can use the above formula to determine that a 9 percent moving average is equivalent to a 21-day exponential moving average:

$$21.2\ days = \left(\frac{2}{0.09}\right) - 1$$

The formula for converting time periods to exponential percentages is:

$$Exponential\ Percentage = \frac{2}{Time\ Periods + 1}$$

You can use the above formula to determine that a 21-day exponential moving average is actually a 9 percent moving average:

$$0.09 = \frac{2}{21 + 1}$$

TRIANGULAR

Triangular moving averages place the majority of the weight on the middle portion of the price series. They are actually double-smoothed simple moving averages. The periods used in the simple moving averages vary, depending on if you specify an odd or even number of time periods.

The following steps explain how to calculate a 12-period triangular moving average.

1. Add 1 to the number of periods in the moving average (e.g., 12 plus 1 is 13).

2. Divide the sum from Step 1 by 2 (e.g., 13 divided by 2 is 6.5).

3. If the result of Step 2 contains a fractional portion, round the result up to the nearest integer (e.g., round 6.5 up to 7).

4. Using the value from Step 3 (i.e., 7), calculate a simple moving average of the closing prices (i.e., a 7-period simple moving average).

5. Again using the value from Step 3 (i.e., 7) calculate a simple moving average of the moving average calculated in Step 4 (i.e., a moving average of a moving average).

VARIABLE

A variable moving average is an exponential moving average that automatically adjusts the smoothing percentage based on the volatility of the data series. The more volatile the data, the more sensitive the smoothing constant used in the moving average calculation. Sensitivity is increased by giving more weight to the current data.

Most moving average calculation methods are unable to compensate for trading range versus trending markets. During trading ranges (when prices move sideways in a narrow range) shorter-term moving averages tend to produce numerous false signals. In trending markets (when prices move up or down over an extended period) longer-term moving averages are slow to react to reversals in trend. By automatically adjusting the smoothing constant, a variable moving average is able to adjust its sensitivity, allowing it to perform better in both types of markets.

A variable moving average is calculated as follows:

(0.078 (VR) * Close) + (1 - 0.078 (VR) * Yesterday's Moving Avg.)

Where:

VR = The Volatility Ratio

Different indicators have been used for the Volatility Ratio. I use a ratio of the VHF indicator (see page 301) compared to the VHF indicator 12 periods ago. The higher this ratio, the "trendier" the market, thereby increasing the sensitivity of the moving average.

The variable moving average was defined by Tushar Chande in an article that appeared in *Technical Analysis of Stocks and Commodities* in March 1992.

WEIGHTED

A weighted moving average is designed to put more weight on recent data and less weight on past data. A weighted moving average is calculated by multiplying each of the previous day's data by a weight. Table 8 shows the calculation of a five-day weighted moving average.

TABLE 8

5-DAY WEIGHTED MOVING AVERAGE									
DAY #	WEIGHT		PRICE		WEIGHTED				AVERAGE
1	1	*	25.00	=	25.00				
2	2	*	26.00	=	52.00				
3	3	*	28.00	=	84.00				
4	4	*	25.00	=	100.00				
5	5	*	29.00	=	145.00				
Totals:	15	*	133.00	=	406.00	/	15	=	27.067

The weight is based on the number of days in the moving average. In the above example, the weight on the first day is 1.0, while the value on the most recent day is 5.0. This gives five times more weight to today's price than the price five days ago.

The following chart displays 25-day moving averages using the simple, exponential, weighted, triangular, and variable methods of calculation.

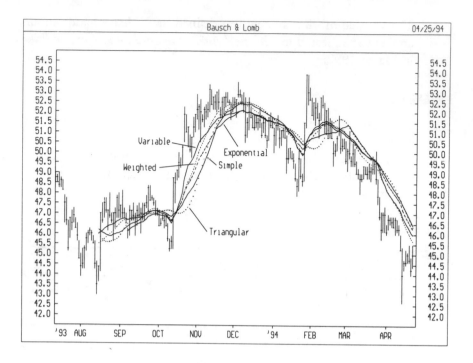

NEGATIVE VOLUME INDEX

OVERVIEW

The Negative Volume Index (NVI) focuses on days when the volume decreases from the previous day. The premise being that the "smart money" takes positions on days when volume decreases.

INTERPRETATION

The interpretation of the NVI assumes that on days when volume increases, the crowd-following "uninformed" investors are in the market. Conversely, on days with decreased volume, the "smart money" is quietly taking positions. Thus, the NVI displays what the smart money is doing.

In *Stock Market Logic,* Norman Fosback points out that the odds of a bull market are 95 out of 100 when the NVI rises above its one-year moving average. The odds of a bull market are roughly 50/50 when the NVI is below its one-year average. Therefore, the NVI is most useful as a bull market indicator.

EXAMPLE

The following chart shows Avon and its NVI. I drew "buy" arrows whenever the NVI crossed above its one-year (255-trading-day) moving average. I drew "equal signs" when the NVI fell below the moving average. You can see that the NVI did a great job of identifying profitable opportunities.

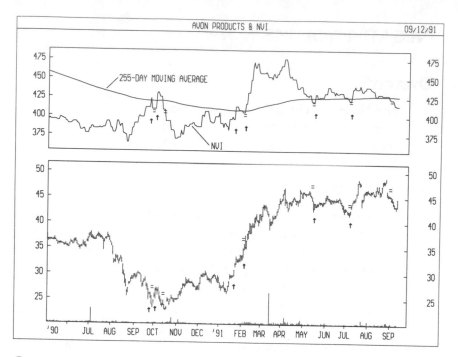

CALCULATION

If today's volume is less than yesterday's volume then:

$$NVI = Yesterday's\ NVI + \left(\frac{Close - Yesterday's\ Close}{Yesterday's\ Close} * Yesterday's\ NVI \right)$$

If today's volume is greater than or equal to yesterday's volume then:

$$NVI = Yesterday's\ NVI$$

Because falling prices are usually associated with falling volume, the NVI usually trends downward.

New Highs-Lows Cumulative

Overview

The New Highs-Lows Cumulative indicator is a long-term market momentum indicator. It is a cumulative total of the difference between the number of stocks reaching new 52-week highs and the number of stocks reaching new 52-week lows.

Interpretation

The New High-Lows Cumulative indicator provides a confirmation of the current trend. Most of the time, the indicator will move in the same direction as major market indices. However, when the indicator and market move in opposite directions, it is likely that the market will reverse.

The interpretation of the New Highs-Lows Cumulative indicator is similar to the Advance/Decline Line in that divergences occur when the indicator fails to confirm the market index's high or low. Divergences (see page 35) during an uptrending market indicate potential weakness, while divergences in a downtrending market indicate potential strength.

Example

The following chart shows the S&P 500 and the New Highs-Lows Cumulative indicator. A classic divergence occurred during 1985 and 1986, when the S&P 500 Index was making new highs but the New Highs-Lows Cumulative indicator was failing to surpass its previous highs. This was followed by the crash of 1987.

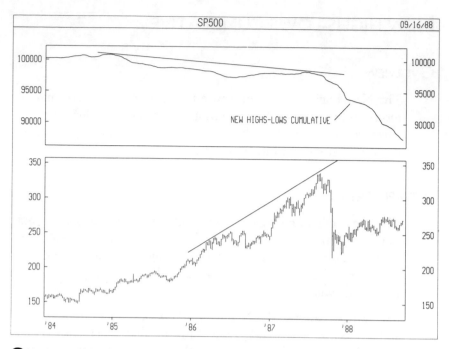

CALCULATION

The New Highs-Lows Cumulative indicator is simply a cumulative total of the number of stocks making new 52-week highs minus the number of stocks making new 52-week lows.

(New Highs – New Lows) + Yesterday's Indicator Value)

NEW HIGHS-NEW LOWS

OVERVIEW

The New Highs-New Lows indicator (NH-NL) displays the daily difference between the number of stocks reaching new 52-week highs and the number of stocks reaching new 52-week lows.

INTERPRETATION

You can interpret the NH-NL indicator as a divergence indicator or as an oscillator. I usually plot a 10-day moving average of the NH-NL indicator to smooth the daily values.

DIVERGENCE

The NH-NL indicator generally reaches its extreme lows slightly before a major market bottom. As the market then turns up from the major bottom, the indicator jumps up rapidly. During this period, many new stocks are making new highs because it's easy to make a new high when prices have been depressed for a long time.

As the cycle matures, a divergence often occurs as fewer and fewer stocks are making new highs (the indicator falls), yet the market indices continue to reach new highs. This is a classic bearish divergence that indicates that the current upward trend is weak and may reverse.

OSCILLATOR

The NH-NL indicator oscillates around zero. If the indicator is positive, the bulls are in control. If it is negative, the bears are in control. You can trade the NH-NL indicator by buying and selling as the indicator passes through zero. This won't always keep you on the right side of the market, but it is helpful to confirm the current trend.

EXAMPLE

The following chart shows the S&P 500 and a 10-day moving average of the NH-NL indicator. I used the NH-NL indicator to confirm a traditional moving average trading system. I drew "buy" arrows when the S&P 500 rose above its 50-day moving average, but only if the 10-day moving average of the NH-NL indicator was above zero. I drew "sell" arrows anytime the S&P 500 fell below its moving average.

By ignoring buy signals unless the 10-day moving average of the NH-NL indicator was above zero, I reduced the number of trades by 50 percent and increased profits by 9 percent.

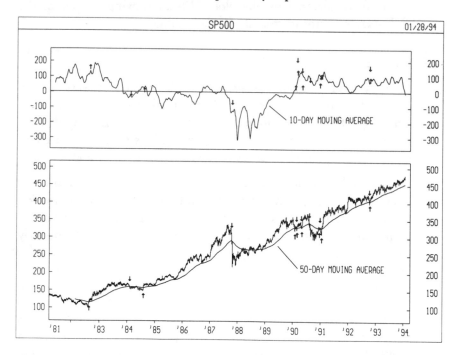

CALCULATION

The New Highs-New Lows is calculated by simply taking the difference between the number of stocks that made new 52-week highs and the number of stocks that made new 52-week lows. I usually plot a 10-day moving average of this value.

New Highs – New Lows

New Highs/Lows Ratio

Overview

The New Highs/Lows Ratio ("NH/NL Ratio") displays the daily ratio between the number of stocks reaching new 52-week highs and the number of stocks reaching new 52-week lows.

Interpretation

The NH/NL Ratio is another useful method of visualizing the relationship of stocks that are making new highs and new lows. High readings indicate that a large number of stocks are making new highs (compared to the number of stocks making new lows). Readings less than 1 indicate that the number of stocks making new highs are less than the number of stocks making lows.

Refer to the New Highs-New Lows indicator (see page 197) for more information on interpreting the NH/NL Ratio.

Example

The following chart shows the S&P 500 and the NH/NL Ratio. The Ratio increased dramatically when the S&P 500 began making new highs in 1990. However, as the S&P has continued to move on to new highs, the ratio has failed to reach new highs. This implies that the S&P 500 is weaker than it appears.

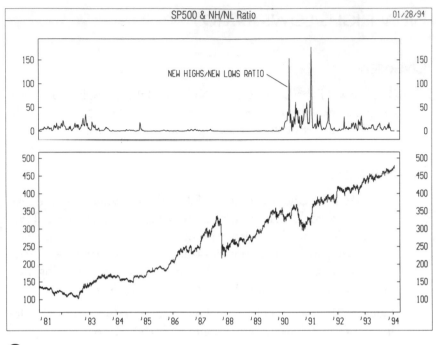

| SP500 & NH/NL Ratio | 01/28/94 |

NEW HIGHS/NEW LOWS RATIO

CALCULATION

$$\frac{Number\ of\ New\ Highs}{Number\ of\ New\ Lows}$$

ODD LOT BALANCE INDEX

OVERVIEW

The Odd Lot Balance Index (OLBI) is a market sentiment indicator that shows the ratio of odd-lot sales to purchases (an "odd lot" is a stock transaction of less than 100 shares). The assumption is that the "odd lotters," the market's smallest traders, don't know what they are doing.

(Unfortunately, the trading of 99-share lots in an effort to skirt the "up-tick" rule, which requires that specialists take short positions only when prices move upward, has rendered odd-lot indicators less reliable.)

INTERPRETATION

When the Odd Lot Balance Index is high, odd lotters are selling more than they are buying and are therefore bearish on the market. To trade contrarily to the odd lotters, you should buy when they are selling (as indicated by a high OLBI) and sell when the odd lotters are bullish and buying (as indicated by a low OLBI).

You can smooth day-to-day fluctuations of the Odd Lot Balance Index by plotting a 10-day moving average of the Index.

EXAMPLE

The following chart shows the S&P 500 (lower window) and a 10-day moving average of the Odd Lot Balance Index (upper window). I drew a vertical line when the odd lotters were excessively pessimistic—which turned out to be a good time to buy.

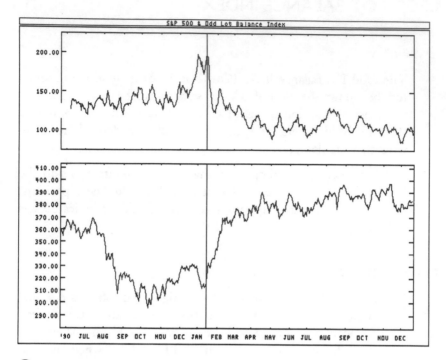

S&P 500 & Odd Lot Balance Index

CALCULATION

$$\left(\frac{Odd\ Lot\ Sales}{Odd\ Lot\ Purchases} \right) * 100$$

ODD LOT PURCHASES/SALES

OVERVIEW

Both of these indicators, Odd Lot Purchases and Odd Lot Sales, display what their names imply: the number of shares (in thousands) purchased or sold in odd lots. An "odd lot" is a stock transaction of less than 100 shares.

(Unfortunately, the trading of 99-share lots in an effort to skirt the "up-tick" rule, which requires that specialists take short positions only when prices move upward, has rendered odd-lot indicators less reliable.)

INTERPRETATION

The odd-lot trade numbers are used in several different ratios and indicators. By themselves, they show the investment activities of the odd-lot traders. Being a contrarian indicator, a high number of Odd Lot Purchases is generally considered bearish, whereas a high number of Odd Lot Sales is considered bullish. The idea is to act opposite of the small, uninformed odd-lot traders.

However, it has been my experience that, for whatever reason, the odd lotters have tended to be on the right side of the market recently.

EXAMPLE

The following chart shows the Value Line Composite Index (lower window) and a 10-day moving average of Odd Lot Sales (upper window). I drew vertical lines when the odd lotters were selling (as identified by relatively high moving average values). Conventional odd-lot interpretation would have you buy at these points. However, in retrospect, it appears that these were appropriate short-term selling points.

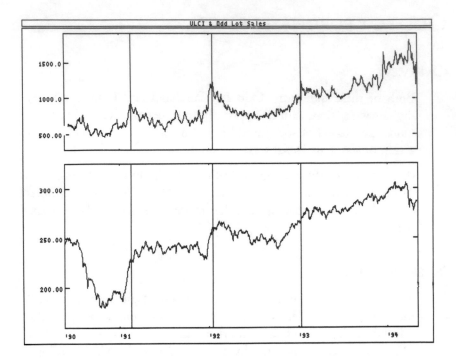

ODD LOT SHORT RATIO

OVERVIEW

The Odd Lot Short Ratio (OLSR) is a market sentiment indicator that displays the daily ratio of odd-lot short sales compared to odd-lot buy/sell transactions.

Investors "short" a stock in anticipation of the stock's price falling. Instead of the traditional transaction of buying at a lower price and profiting by selling at a higher price, the short sale transaction is just the opposite. To profit from a short sale, the stock must be sold at a higher price and bought (covered) at a lower price. An "odd-lot" short is a short sale transaction involving less than 100 shares.

INTERPRETATION

If we could find an investor who was always wrong and do the exact opposite of him, we would always be right! Odd-lot indicators strive to do just that. If we assume that small investors ("odd lotters") are inexperienced (and thus usually wrong), then trading contrarily to the odd-lot traders should be profitable.

The higher the OLSR indicator, the higher the percentage of odd-lot shorts and the more likely it is that the market will rise (proving the odd lotters wrong). Similarly, the lower the OLSR, the more likely it is that a market decline will occur.

Generally, this rule (invest contrarily to the odd lotters) has held true. Odd lotters tend to be reactive rather than proactive. High Odd Lot Short Ratios tend to come after major market declines (when investors should be buying, not selling) and low readings usually come after long market advances.

In 1986, the number of odd-lot shorts reached levels that were unheard of. The explanation I have heard for this is that specialists are placing multiple odd-lot short orders to avoid the up-tick rule, which states that a short order must be processed on an up-tick. They do this on days with major declines in prices.

If this explanation is true, it drastically complicates the interpretation of all odd-lot indicators. It would mean that the odd-lot indicators show what the "littlest" guy is doing, except when it reaches extreme readings, in which case it would show what the "biggest" guy (the Members) is doing.

EXAMPLE

Refer to the examples on pages 201 and 203.

CALCULATION

The Odd Lot Short Ratio is calculated by dividing the number of odd-lot short sales by the average number of odd-lot transactions for the day. (Because odd lots do not necessarily have a buyer and a seller for every transaction, we calculate the average number of transactions by adding the number of odd-lot buy orders to the number of odd-lot sell orders and then dividing by two.)

$$\left(\frac{Odd\ Lot\ Shorts}{\left(\frac{Odd\ Lot\ Purchases\ +\ Odd\ Lot\ Sales}{2} \right)} \right) * 100$$

ON BALANCE VOLUME

OVERVIEW

On Balance Volume (OBV) is a momentum indicator that relates volume to price change.

On Balance Volume was developed by Joe Granville and was originally presented in his book *New Strategy of Daily Stock Market Timing for Maximum Profits.*

INTERPRETATION

On Balance Volume is a running total of volume. It shows if volume is flowing into or out of a security. When the security closes higher than the previous close, all of the day's volume is considered up-volume. When the security closes lower than the previous close, all of the day's volume is considered down-volume.

A full explanation of OBV is beyond the scope of this book. If you would like further information on OBV analysis, I recommend that you read Granville's book, *New Strategy of Daily Stock Market Timing for Maximum Profits.*

The basic assumption regarding OBV analysis is that OBV changes precede price changes. The theory is that smart money can be seen flowing into the security by a rising OBV. When the public then moves into the security, both the security and the OBV will surge ahead.

If the security's price movement precedes OBV movement, a "nonconfirmation" has occurred. Nonconfirmations can occur at bull market tops (when the security rises without, or before, the OBV) or at bear market bottoms (when the security falls without, or before, the OBV).

The OBV is in a rising trend when each new peak is higher than the previous peak and each new trough is higher than the previous trough. Likewise, the OBV is in a falling trend when each successive peak is lower than the previous peak and each successive trough is lower than the previous trough. When the OBV is moving sideways and is not making successive highs and lows, it is in a doubtful trend. [See Figure 47]

FIGURE 47

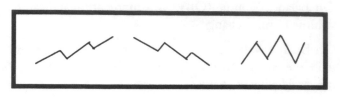

Up Trend   Down Trend   Doubtful Trend

Once a trend is established, it remains in force until it is broken. There are two ways in which the OBV trend can be broken. The first occurs when the trend changes from a rising trend to a falling trend, or from a falling trend to a rising trend.

The second way the OBV trend can be broken is if the trend changes to a doubtful trend and remains doubtful for more than three days. Thus, if the security changes from a rising trend to a doubtful trend and remains doubtful for only two days before changing back to a rising trend, the OBV is considered to have always been in a rising trend.

When the OBV changes to a rising or falling trend, a "breakout" has occurred. Since OBV breakouts normally precede price breakouts, investors should buy long on OBV upside breakouts. Likewise, investors should sell short when the OBV makes a downside breakout. Positions should be held until the trend changes (as explained in the preceding paragraph).

This method of analyzing On Balance Volume is designed for trading short-term cycles. According to Granville, investors must act quickly and decisively if they wish to profit from short-term OBV analysis.

EXAMPLE

The following chart shows PepsiCo and the On Balance Volume indicator. I have labeled the OBV Up, Down, and Doubtful trends.

A falling trend, as you will recall, is defined by lower peaks and lower troughs. Conversely, a rising trend is defined by higher peaks and higher troughs.

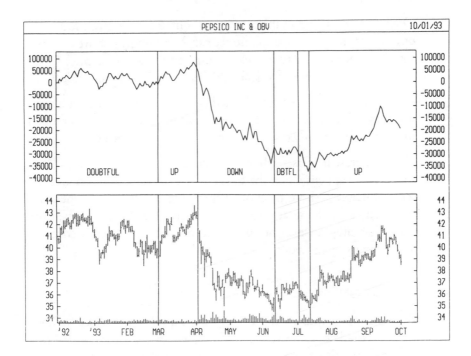

CALCULATION

On Balance Volume is calculated by adding the day's volume to a cumulative total when the security's price closes up, and subtracting the day's volume when the security's price closes down.

If today's close is greater than yesterday's close, then:

$$OBV = Yesterday's\ OBV + Today's\ Volume$$

If today's close is less than yesterday's close, then:

$$OBV = Yesterday's\ OBV - Today's\ Volume$$

If today's close is equal to yesterday's close, then:

$$OBV = Yesterday's\ OBV$$

Open Interest

Overview

Open Interest is the number of open contracts of a given future or option contract. An open contract can be a long or short contract that has not been exercised, closed out, or allowed to expire. Open interest is really more of a data field (see page 7) than an indicator.

A fact that is sometimes overlooked is that a futures contract always involves a buyer and a seller. This means that one unit of open interest always represents two people, a buyer and a seller.

Open interest increases when a buyer and seller create a new contract. This happens when the buyer initiates a long position and the seller initiates a short position. Open interest decreases when the buyer and seller liquidate existing contracts. This happens when the buyer is selling an existing long position and the seller is covering an existing short position.

Interpretation

By itself, open interest shows only the liquidity of a specific contract or market. However, combining volume analysis with open interest sometimes provides subtle clues to the flow of money in and out of the market:

- Rising volume and rising open interest confirm the direction of the current trend.

- Falling volume and falling open interest signal that an end to the current trend may be imminent.

Example

The following chart shows copper, open interest (the solid line), and volume (the dotted line). The open interest is for all copper contracts, not just the current contract.

I drew a trendline (A) when both open interest and volume were increasing. This confirmed the upward trend of prices as shown by the trendline (B).

I then drew a vertical line (C) when open interest and volume began to diverge. From this point, volume continued to increase while open interest decreased sharply. This warned of an end to the rising trend.

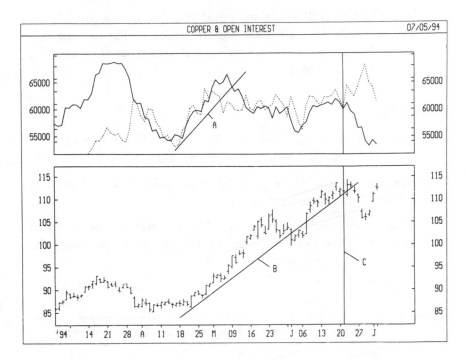

Open-10 TRIN

Overview

The Open-10 TRIN is a smoothed variation of the Arms Index (see page 67). It is a market breadth indicator that uses advancing/declining volume and advancing/declining issues to measure the strength of the market.

Interpretation

The interpretation of Open-10 TRIN (also called the Open Trading Index) is similar to the interpretation of the "normal" TRIN.

Readings above 0.90 are generally considered bearish and readings below 0.90 are considered bullish.

Table 9 was reprinted from Peter Eliades' *Stock Market Cycles*. It shows what the DJIA did after the 10-day TRIN rose above the level of one. Impressive . . .

Table 9

1st reading > 1.0	Days to final low	Next market move
May 23, 1984	3	60-point rally
June 15, 1984	1	63-point rally
July 20, 1984	3	165-point rally
October 10, 1984	0	88-point rally
November 16, 1984	1	45-point rally
December 5, 1984	3	69-point rally
January 3, 1985	1	130-point rally
March 15, 1985	1	48-point rally
April 30, 1985	2	96-point rally
June 19, 1985	3	78-point rally

I created a similar table (Table 10) for the period 1985 through 1989.

TABLE 10

1ST READING > 1.0	DAYS TO FINAL LOW	NEXT MARKET MOVE
June 19, 1985	0	60-point rally
January 8, 1986	2	302-point rally
April 30, 1986	N/A	16-point rally
July 15, 1986	0	41-point rally
September 11, 1986	1	141-point rally
January 2, 1987	0	445-point rally
October 15, 1987	2	289-point rally
November 13, 1987	4	68-point rally
November 27, 1987	5	285-point rally
January 14, 1988	5	285-point rally
February 8, 1988	5	79-point rally
March 11, 1988	0	53-point rally
April 4, 1988	0	127-point rally
May 12, 1988	0	39-point rally
May 17, 1988	4	211-point rally
July 1, 1988	N/A	78-point rally
August 12, 1988	7	111-point rally
November 16, 1988	0	309-point rally
October 30, 1989	5	171-point rally
December 18, 1989	2	109-point rally

CALCULATION

The Open-10 TRIN is calculated by keeping a 10-day total of each of the TRIN's components before performing the TRIN calculation.

$$\frac{\left(\dfrac{10 - \textit{Period Total of Advancing Issues}}{10 - \textit{Period Total of Declining Issues}} \right)}{\left(\dfrac{10 - \textit{Period Total of Advancing Volume}}{10 - \textit{Period Total of Declining Volume}} \right)}$$

OPTION ANALYSIS

OVERVIEW

The most widely used option pricing model is the Black-Scholes option valuation model, which was developed by Fisher Black and Myron Scholes in 1973.

The Black-Scholes model helps determine the fair market value of an option based on the security's price and volatility, time until expiration, and the current market interest rate. The following assumptions were made by Black and Scholes when the model was developed:

1. Markets are "frictionless." In other words, there are no transaction costs or taxes; all market participants may borrow and lend at the "riskless" rate of interest; there are no penalties for short selling; and all securities are infinitely divisible (i.e., fractional shares can be purchased).

2. Stock prices are lognormally distributed (i.e., they follow a bell curve). This means that a stock can double in price as easily as it can drop to half its price.

3. Stocks do not pay dividends or make any distributions. (The model is often modified to allow for dividend adjustments.)

4. The option can be exercised only on the expiration date.

The components of the option model are security price, volatility, option life, market interest rate, and dividend (if any).

I suggest you refer to the book *Option Volatility and Pricing Strategies,* by Sheldon Natenberg, for more information on calculations and strategies using the Black-Scholes model.

INTERPRETATION

PUT/CALL PRICE

The Put/Call Price is the main output of the Black-Scholes model. It shows how much an option should sell for based on the various components that make up the model (e.g., volatility, option life, security price, etc). It helps answer the question, "Is the option overpriced or underpriced?"

The usefulness of the Put/Call Price is basically twofold:

1. It helps you locate mispriced options. The option purchaser can use the model to find options that are underpriced. The option writer can use the model to find options that are overpriced.

2. It helps you form a riskless hedge to earn arbitrage profits. For example, you could buy undervalued calls and then short the underlying stock. This creates a riskless hedge because regardless of whether the security's price goes up or down, the two positions will exactly offset each other. You would then wait for the option to return to its fair market value to earn arbitrage profits.

Delta (below) is used to determine the number of shares to purchase in order to form a riskless hedge.

DELTA

Delta shows the amount that the option's price will change if the underlying security's price changes by $1.00.

For example, if XYZ is selling for $25.00/share, a call option on XYZ is selling for $2.00 and the Delta is 75 percent, then the option's price should increase $0.75 (to $2.75) if the price of XYZ increases to $26.00/share. In other words, the option should go up $0.75 for each $1.00 that XYZ goes up.

If an option is deep in-the-money, then it will have a high Delta, because almost all of the gain/loss in the security will be reflected in the option price. Conversely, deep out-of-the-money options will have a low Delta, because very little of the gain/loss in the security is reflected in the option price.

If you don't have a computer, the rough rule of thumb for calculating Delta is: 75 percent for an option $5.00 in the money, 50 percent for an option at the money, and 25 percent for an option $5.00 out of the money.

As an in-the-money option nears expiration, the Delta will approach 100 percent because the amount of time remaining for the option to move out-of-the-money is small.

Delta is also used to determine the correct number of shares to buy/short to form a "riskless hedge." For example, suppose the Delta on a put option is 66 percent. A riskless hedge would result from owning a ratio of two-thirds (66 percent) a position in stock (i.e., 66 shares) to every one long position in a put option contract. If the stock price goes up one point, then the stock position will increase $66.00. This $66.00 increase should be exactly offset by a $66.00 decrease in the value of the put option contract.

As discussed on page 215, forming a riskless hedge gives the investor the potential of earning arbitrage profits by profiting from the undervalued option's return to its fair market value (i.e., the price at which the option is neither overpriced nor underpriced). Theoretically, the market will eventually value underpriced options at their fair market value. However, it should be noted that high transaction costs may undermine this theory.

GAMMA

Gamma shows the anticipated change in Delta, given a one-point increase in the underlying security. Thus, it shows how responsive Delta is to a change in the underlying security's price. For example, a Gamma of four indicates that the Delta will increase four points (e.g., from 50 percent to 54 percent) for each one-point increase in the underlying security's price.

Gamma indicates the amount of risk involved with an option position. A large Gamma indicates higher risk, because the value of the option can change more quickly. However, a trader may desire higher risk depending on the strategy employed.

OPTION LIFE

Option Life shows the number of days until expiration. Generally speaking, the longer the time until expiration, the more valuable the option.

A graph of Option Life appears as a stepped line from the upper-left to the lower-right side of the screen. The reason the line is stepped is because of weekends and holidays. For example, on Friday there may be 146 days to expiration and on the following Monday only 143 days remaining.

THETA

Theta shows the change in the option's price (in points) due to the effect of time alone. The longer the time until expiration, the less effect that time has on the price of the option. However, as the option nears expiration, the effect can be great, particularly on out-of-the-money options. Theta is also referred to as "time decay."

For example, a Theta value of -0.0025 means that the option lost 1/4 of one cent due to the passage of time alone.

The effect of time on the option price is almost always positive. The more time until expiration the better chance the option has of being in-the-money at expiration. The only exception to this positive relationship is deep in-the-money put options with an expiration date far into the future.

All other things being equal, options with low Thetas are more preferable (for purchase) than are those with high Thetas.

VEGA

Vega shows the change in the option price due to an assumed 1 percent increase in the underlying security's volatility. Vega shows the dollar amount of gain that should be expected if the volatility goes up one point (all else being equal).

The effect of volatility on the option price is always positive. The greater the volatility of the underlying security, the better chance the option has of being in-the-money at expiration. Therefore, options with higher volatilities will cost more than those with lower volatilities.

Since Vega measures the sensitivity of an option to a change in volatility, options with higher Vegas are more preferable (for purchase) than those with low Vegas.

VOLATILITY

Volatility is a measurement that shows the degree of fluctuation that a security experiences over a given time frame. Wide price movements over a short time frame are characteristic of high volatility stocks.

Volatility is the only input parameter of the Black-Scholes model (e.g., security price, volatility, option life, market interest rate) that is calculated, yet the accuracy of the model is highly dependent on a good Volatility figure. The best measurement of volatility is the one that captures future price movements. But if we knew what future price movements would be, we would care less about the Black-Scholes model—we'd be trading! However, reality forces us to estimate volatility. There are two ways to estimate volatility for use with the Black-Scholes model: Historical Volatility and Implied Volatility.

Historical Volatility measures the actual volatility of the security's prices using a standard-deviation-based formula. It shows how volatile prices have been over the last *x* time periods. The advantage of historical volatility is that it can be calculated using only historical security prices. When you calculate the Black-Scholes put/call price using historical volatility, most options appear overpriced.

A more widely used measure of option volatility is called *Implied Volatility.* Implied Volatility is the amount of volatility that the option market is assuming (i.e., implying) for the option. To calculate implied volatility, the actual option price, security price, strike price, and the option expiration date are plugged into the Black-Scholes formula. The formula then solves for the implied volatility.

Options of high volatility stocks are worth more (i.e., carry higher premiums) than those with low volatility, because of the greater chance the option has of moving in-the-money by expiration. Option purchasers normally prefer options with high volatilities and option writers normally prefer options with low volatilities (all else being equal).

CALCULATION

For exact mathematical formulas used in calculating option values, I recommend *Option Volatility and Pricing Strategies,* by Sheldon Natenberg.

The formula for the Black-Scholes option pricing model is widely available in many books and publications. The original work by Black and Scholes was done only on equity call options. Since their work was originally published, extensions of their model have been developed, such as models for put options and options on futures. Gamma, Theta, and Vega calculations are all extensions of the original Black-Scholes model.

Adjusting the model for dividends provides a more accurate calculation of the option's fair market value. A popular adjustment method assumes that dividend payments are paid out continuously.

OVERBOUGHT/OVERSOLD

OVERVIEW

The Overbought/Oversold (OB/OS) indicator is a market breadth indicator based on the smoothed difference between advancing and declining issues.

INTERPRETATION

The OB/OS indicator shows when the stock market is overbought (and a correction is due) and when it is oversold (and a rally is due).

Readings above +200 are generally considered bearish and readings below −200 are generally considered bullish. When the OB/OS indicator falls below +200 a sell signal is generated. Similarly, a buy signal is generated when the OB/OS indicator rises above −200.

As with all OB/OS-type indicators, extreme readings may be a sign of a change in investor expectations and may not be followed by the expected correction. (Refer to the discussion on the Advance/Decline Ratio, page 59, and the McClellan Oscillator, page 171, for additional comments on extremely overbought/oversold conditions.)

EXAMPLE

The following chart shows the DJIA and the Overbought/Oversold indicator. I drew "buy" and "sell" arrows when the indicator penetrated the +200/−200 levels. The OB/OS indicator works very well in this type of trading-range market.

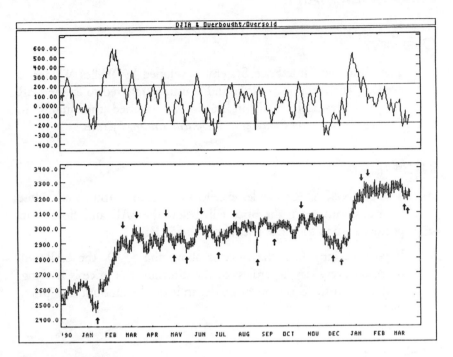

CALCULATION

The Overbought/Oversold indicator is a 10-period exponential moving average of the difference between the number of advancing and declining issues.

10-period moving average of (Advancing Issues – Declining Issues)

PARABOLIC SAR

OVERVIEW

The Parabolic Time/Price System, developed by Welles Wilder, is used to set trailing price stops and is usually referred to as the SAR (stop-and-reversal). This indicator is explained thoroughly in Wilder's book, *New Concepts in Technical Trading Systems.*

INTERPRETATION

The Parabolic SAR provides excellent exit points. You should close long positions when the price falls below the SAR and close short positions when the price rises above the SAR.

If you are long (i.e., the price is above the SAR), the SAR will move up every day, regardless of the direction the price is moving. The amount the SAR moves up depends on the amount that prices move.

EXAMPLE

The following chart shows Compaq and its Parabolic SAR. You should be long when the SAR is below prices and short when it is above prices.

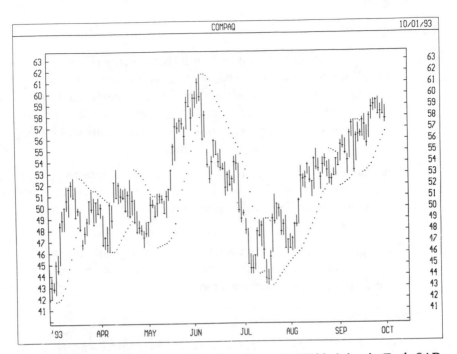

The Parabolic SAR is plotted as shown in Wilder's book. Each SAR stop level point is displayed on the day on which it is in effect. Note that the SAR value is today's, not tomorrow's, stop level.

CALCULATION

It is beyond the scope of this book to explain the calculation of the Parabolic SAR. Refer to Wilder's book, *New Concepts in Technical Trading*, for detailed calculation information.

PATTERNS

OVERVIEW

A basic principle of technical analysis is that security prices move in trends. We also know that trends do not last forever. They eventually change direction, and when they do, they rarely do so on a dime. Instead, prices typically decelerate, pause, and then reverse. These phases occur as investors form new expectations and by doing so, shift the security's supply/demand lines.

The changing of expectations often causes price patterns to emerge. Although no two markets are identical, their price patterns are often very similar. Predictable price behavior often follows these price patterns.

Chart patterns can last from a few days to many months or even years. Generally speaking, the longer a pattern takes to form, the more dramatic the ensuing price move.

INTERPRETATION

The following sections explain some of the more common price patterns. For more information on chart patterns, I suggest the book *Technical Analysis of Stock Trends* by Robert Edwards and John Magee.

HEAD-AND-SHOULDERS

The Head-and-Shoulders price pattern is the most reliable and well-known chart pattern. It gets its name from its resemblance to a head with two shoulders on either side. The reason this reversal pattern is so common is due to the manner in which trends typically reverse.

A uptrend is formed as prices make higher-highs and higher-lows in a stair-step fashion. The trend is broken when this upward climb ends. As you can see in the following illustration, the "left shoulder" and the "head" are the last two higher-highs. The right shoulder is created as the bulls try to push prices higher, but are unable to do so. This signifies the end of the uptrend. Confirmation of a new downtrend occurs when the "neckline" is penetrated.

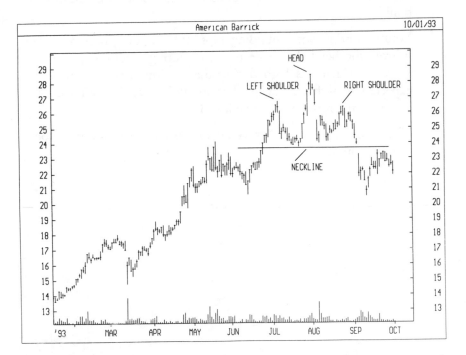

During a healthy uptrend, volume should increase during each rally. A sign that the trend is weakening occurs when the volume accompanying rallies is less than the volume accompanying the preceding rally. In a typical Head-and-Shoulders pattern, volume decreases on the head and is especially light on the right shoulder.

Following the penetration of the neckline, it is very common for prices to return to the neckline in a last effort to continue the uptrend (as shown in the preceding chart). If prices are then unable to rise above the neckline, they usually decline rapidly on increased volume.

An inverse (or upside-down) Head-and-Shoulders pattern often coincides with market bottoms. As with a normal Head-and-Shoulders pattern, volume usually decreases as the pattern is formed and then increases as prices rise above the neckline.

ROUNDING TOPS AND BOTTOMS

Rounding tops occur as expectations gradually shift from bullish to bearish. The gradual, yet steady shift forms a rounded top. Rounding bottoms occur as expectations gradually shift from bearish to bullish.

Volume during both rounding tops and rounding bottoms often mirrors the bowl-like shape of prices during a rounding bottom. Volume, which was high during the previous trend, decreases as expectations shift and traders become indecisive. Volume then increases as the new trend is established.

The following chart shows Goodyear and a classic rounding bottom formation.

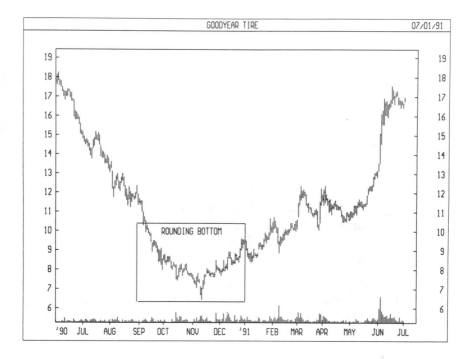

TRIANGLES

A triangle occurs as the range between peaks and troughs narrows. Triangles typically occur as prices encounter a support or resistance level that constricts the prices.

A "symmetrical triangle" occurs when prices are making both lower-highs and higher-lows. An "ascending triangle" occurs when there are higher-lows (as with a symmetrical triangle), but the highs are occurring at the same price level due to resistance. The odds favor an upside breakout from an ascending triangle. A "descending triangle" occurs when there are lower-highs (as with a symmetrical triangle), but the lows are occurring at the same price level due to support. The odds favor a downside breakout from a descending triangle.

Just as pressure increases when water is forced through a narrow opening, the "pressure" of prices increases as the triangle pattern forms. Prices will usually break out rapidly from a triangle. Breakouts are confirmed when they are accompanied by an increase in volume.

The most reliable breakouts occur somewhere between half and three-quarters of the distance between the beginning and end (apex) of the triangle. There are seldom many clues as to the direction prices will break out of a symmetrical triangle. If prices move all the way through the triangle to the apex, a breakout is unlikely.

The following chart shows Boeing and a descending triangle. Note the strong downside breakout on increased volume.

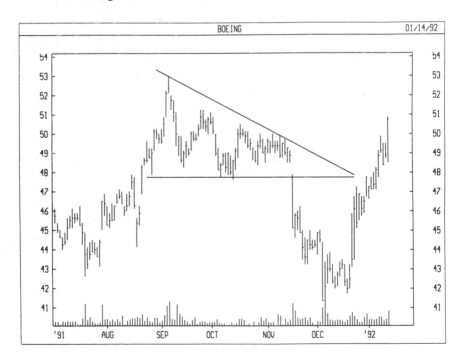

DOUBLE TOPS AND BOTTOMS

A double top occurs when prices rise to a resistance level on significant volume, retreat, and subsequently return to the resistance level on decreased volume. Prices then decline, marking the beginning of a new downtrend.

A double bottom has the same characteristics as a double top except it is upside-down.

The following chart shows Caterpillar and a double bottom pattern.

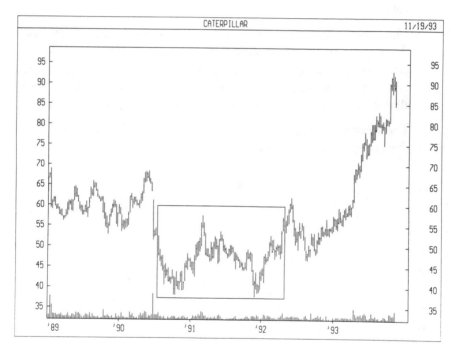

Percent retracement

Overview

A characteristic of a healthy bull market is that it makes higher-highs and higher-lows. This indicates a continual upward shift in expectations and the supply/demand lines. The amount that prices retreat following a higher-high can be measured using a technique referred to as "percent retracement." This measures the percentage that prices "retraced" from the high to the low.

For example, if a stock moves from a low of 50 to a high of 100 and then retraces to 75, the move from 100 to 75 (25 points) retraced 50 percent of the original move from 50 to 100.

Interpretation

Measuring the percent retracement can be helpful when determining the price levels at which prices will reverse and continue upward. During a vigorous bull market, prices often retrace up to 33 percent of the original move. It is not uncommon for prices to retrace up to 50 percent. Retracements of more than 66 percent almost always signify an end to the bull market.

Some investors feel that the similarities between 33 percent, 50 percent, and 66 percent and the Fibonacci numbers of 38.2 percent, 50 percent, and 61.8 percent are significant. These investors will use Fibonacci Levels (see page 134) to view retracement levels.

Example

I labeled the following chart of Great Western at three points (labeled A, B, and C). These points define the price before the price move (A), at the end of the price move (B), and at the retraced price (C). In this example, prices have retraced 61.5 percent of the original price move.

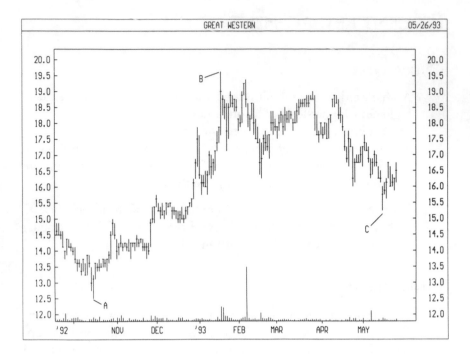

PERFORMANCE

OVERVIEW

The Performance indicator displays a security's price performance as a percentage. This is sometimes called a "normalized" chart.

INTERPRETATION

The Performance indicator displays the percentage that the security has increased since the first period displayed. For example, if the Performance indicator is 10, it means that the security's price has increased 10 percent since the first period displayed on the left side of the chart. Similarly, a value of −10 percent means that the security's price has fallen by 10 percent since the first period displayed.

Performance charts are helpful for comparing the price movements of different securities.

EXAMPLE

The following chart shows United Airlines and its Performance indicator. The indicator shows that United's price has increased 16 percent since the beginning of 1993.

CALCULATION

The Performance indicator is calculated by dividing the change in prices by the first price displayed.

$$\left(\frac{Current\ Close - First\ Close}{First\ Close} \right) * 100$$

POINT AND FIGURE

OVERVIEW

Point and Figure (P&F) charts differ from traditional price charts in that they completely disregard the passage of time and display only changes in prices. Rather than having price on the y-axis and time on the x- axis, P&F charts display price changes on both axes. This is similar to Kagi (see page 158), Renko (see page 258), and Three Line Break (see page 275) charts.

INTERPRETATION

Point and Figure charts display the underlying supply and demand of prices. A column of X's shows that demand is exceeding supply (a rally); a column of O's shows that supply is exceeding demand (a decline); and a series of short columns shows that supply and demand are relatively equal.

There are several chart patterns (see page 224) that regularly appear in P&F charts. These include Double Tops and Bottoms, Bullish and Bearish Signal formations, Bullish and Bearish Symmetrical Triangles, Triple Tops and Bottoms, etc. It is beyond the scope of this book to fully explain all of these patterns.

EXAMPLE

The following two charts both show the prices of Atlantic Richfield. The first chart displays prices in P&F and the second chart displays prices as high, low, close bars.

As I mentioned above, P&F charts focus only on price action. Looking at this P&F chart, you can see that prices were initially contained between a support level at 114 and a resistance level at 121. When prices broke above the resistance level at 121 (the long column of X's), that level became the new support level. This new support level eventually failed (the long column of O's), prices retested the support at 114, made a small rally, and then fell below the 114 support level.

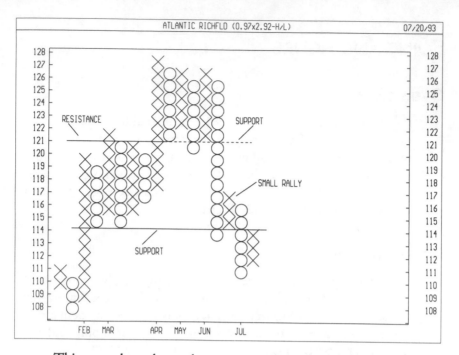

This next chart shows the same pricing information as the preceding P&F chart. You can see that the support and resistance levels are also identifiable in this bar chart, but the P&F chart made it much easier to identify them.

CALCULATION

Point and Figure charts display an "X" when prices rise by the "box size" (a value you specify) and display an "O" when prices fall by the box size. Note that no X's or O's are drawn if prices rise or fall by an amount that is less than the box size.

Each column can contain either X's or O's, but never both. In order to change columns (e.g., from an X column to an O column), prices must reverse by the "reversal amount" (another value you specify) multiplied by the box size. For example, if the box size is three points and the reversal amount is two boxes, then prices must reverse direction six points (three multiplied by two) in order to change columns. If you are in a column of X's, the price must fall six points to change to a column of O's. If you are in a column of O's, the price must rise six points to change to a column of X's.

The changing of columns identifies a change in the trend of prices. When a new column of X's appears, it shows that prices are rallying higher. When a new column of O's appears, it shows that prices are moving lower.

Because prices must reverse direction by the reversal amount, the minimum number of X's or O's that can appear in a column is equal to the "reversal amount."

The common practice is to use the high and low prices (not just the close) to decide if prices have changed enough to display a new box.

POSITIVE VOLUME INDEX

OVERVIEW

The Positive Volume Index (PVI) focuses on days when the volume increased from the previous day. The premise being that the "crowd" takes positions on days when volume increases.

INTERPRETATION

Interpretation of the PVI assumes that on days when volume increases, the crowd-following, "uninformed" investors are in the market. Conversely, on days with decreased volume, the "smart money" is quietly taking positions. Thus, the PVI displays what the not-so-smart money is doing. (The Negative Volume Index, page 193, displays what the smart money is doing.) Note, however, that the PVI is not a contrarian indicator. Even though the PVI is supposed to show what the not-so-smart money is doing, it still trends in the same direction as prices.

Table 11 summarizes NVI and PVI data from 1941 through 1975 as explained in *Stock Market Logic,* by Norman Fosback.

TABLE 11

INDICATOR	INDICATOR RELATIVE TO ONE-YEAR MOVING AVERAGE	PROBABILITY THAT BULL MARKET IS IN PROGRESS	PROBABILITY THAT BEAR MARKET IS IN PROGRESS
NVI	Above	96%	4%
PVI	Above	79%	21%
NVI	Below	47%	53%
PVI	Below	33%	67%

As you can see, NVI is excellent at identifying bull markets (i.e., when the NVI is above its one-year moving average) and the PVI is pretty good at identifying bull markets (when the PVI is above its moving average) and bear markets (i.e., when the PVI is below its moving average).

EXAMPLE

The following chart shows the NVI, the PVI, and the Dow Jones Industrial Average (DJIA) over a four-year period (weekly data). The NVI and PVI indicators are labeled bullish or bearish, depending on if they were above or below their 52-week moving averages.

The DJIA is labeled as Bullish when either the NVI or PVI was above its moving average, and as Very Bullish when both the indicators were above their moving averages.

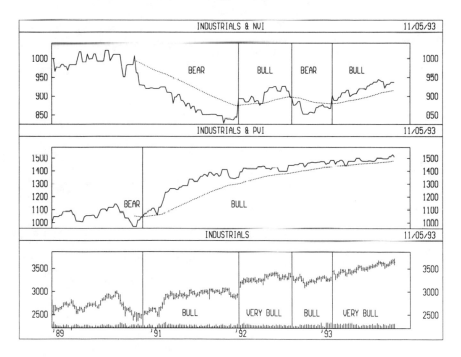

CALCULATION

If today's volume is greater than yesterday's volume, then:

$$PVI = Yesterday's\ PVI + \left(\frac{Close - Yesterday's\ Close}{Yesterday's\ Close} * Yesterday's\ PVI \right)$$

If today's volume is less than or equal to yesterday's volume, then:

$$PVI = \textit{Yesterday's PVI}$$

Because rising prices are usually associated with rising volume, the PVI usually trends upward.

PRICE AND VOLUME TREND

OVERVIEW

The Price and Volume Trend (PVT) is similar to On Balance Volume (OBV, page 207) in that it is a cumulative total of volume that is adjusted depending on changes in closing prices. But where OBV adds all volume on days when prices close higher and subtracts all volume on days when prices close lower, the PVT adds/subtracts only a portion of the daily volume. The amount of volume added to the PVT is determined by the amount that prices rose or fell relative to the previous day's close.

INTERPRETATION

The interpretation of the Price and Volume Trend is similar to the interpretation of On Balance Volume (see page 207) and the Volume Accumulation/Distribution Line (see page 52).

Many investors feel that the PVT more accurately illustrates the flow of money into and out of a security than does OBV. This is because OBV adds the same amount of volume to the indicator regardless of whether the security closes up a fraction of a point or doubles in price. Whereas, the PVT adds only a small portion of volume to the indicator when the price changes by a small percentage and adds a large portion of volume to the indicator when the price changes by a large percentage.

EXAMPLE

The following chart shows Dupont and the PVT. The bullish divergence (the PVT was trending higher while prices trended lower) was followed by a strong price increase.

CALCULATION

The PVT is calculated by multiplying the day's volume by the percent that the security's price changed, and adding this value to a cumulative total.

$$\left(\left(\frac{Close - Yesterday's\ Close}{Yesterday's\ Close} \right) * Volume \right) + Yesterday's\ PVT$$

For example, if the security's price increased 0.5 percent on volume of 10,000 shares, we would add 50 (i.e., 0.005 * 10,000) to the PVT. If the security's price had closed down 0.5 percent, we would have subtracted 50 from the PVT.

PRICE OSCILLATOR

OVERVIEW

The Price Oscillator displays the difference between two moving averages of a security's price. The difference between the moving averages can be expressed in either points or percentages.

The Price Oscillator is almost identical to the MACD (see page 166), except that the Price Oscillator can use any two user-specified moving averages. (The MACD always uses 12- and 26-day moving averages, and always expresses the difference in points.)

INTERPRETATION

Moving average analysis typically generates buy signals when a short-term moving average (or the security's price) rises above a longer-term moving average. Conversely, sell signals are generated when a shorter-term moving average (or the security's price) falls below a longer-term moving average. The Price Oscillator illustrates the cyclical and often profitable signals generated by these one- or two-moving-average systems.

EXAMPLE

The following chart shows Kellogg and a 10-day/30-day Price Oscillator. In this example, the Price Oscillator shows the difference between the moving averages as percentages.

I drew "buy" arrows when the Price Oscillator rose above zero and "sell" arrows when the indicator fell below zero. This example is typical of the Price Oscillator's effectiveness. Because the Price Oscillator is a trend-following indicator, it does an outstanding job of keeping you on the right side of the market during trending periods (as shown by the arrows labeled B, E, and F). However, during less decisive periods, the Price Oscillator produces small losses (as shown by the arrows labeled A, C, and D).

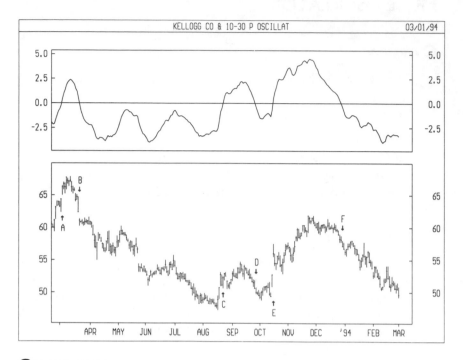

CALCULATION

When the Price Oscillator displays the difference between the moving averages in points, it subtracts the longer-term moving average from the shorter-term average:

Shorter Moving Average - Longer Moving Average

When the Price Oscillator displays the difference between the moving averages in percentages, it divides the difference between the averages by the shorter-term moving average:

$$\left(\frac{\textit{Shorter Moving Average} - \textit{Longer Moving Average}}{\textit{Shorter Moving Average}} \right) * 100$$

PRICE RATE-OF-CHANGE

OVERVIEW

The Price Rate-of-Change (ROC) indicator displays the difference between the current price and the price *x* time periods ago. The difference can be displayed either in points or as a percentage. The Momentum indicator (see page 180) displays the same information, but expresses it as a ratio.

INTERPRETATION

It is a well-recognized phenomenon that security prices surge ahead and retract in a cyclical, wavelike motion. This cyclical action is the result of the changing expectations as bulls and bears struggle to control prices.

The ROC displays the wavelike motion in an oscillator format by measuring the amount that prices have changed over a given time period. As prices increase, the ROC rises; as prices fall, the ROC falls. The greater the change in prices, the greater the change in the ROC.

The time period used to calculate the ROC may range from one day (which results in a volatile chart showing the daily price change) to 200 days (or longer). The most popular time periods are the 12- and 25-day ROC for short- to intermediate-term trading. These time periods were popularized by Gerald Appel and Fred Hitschler in their book, *Stock Market Trading Systems*.

The 12-day ROC is an excellent short- to intermediate-term overbought/oversold indicator. The higher the ROC, the more overbought the security; the lower the ROC, the more likely a rally. However, as with all overbought/oversold indicators, it is prudent to wait for the market to begin to correct (i.e., turn up or down) before placing your trade. A market that appears overbought may remain overbought for some time. In fact, extremely overbought/oversold readings usually imply a *continuation* of the current trend.

The 12-day ROC tends to be very cyclical, oscillating back and forth in a fairly regular cycle. Often, price changes can be anticipated by studying the previous cycles of the ROC and relating the previous cycles to the current market.

EXAMPLE

The following chart shows the 12-day ROC of Walgreen expressed in percent. I drew "buy" arrows each time the ROC fell below, and then rose above, the oversold level of –6.5. I drew "sell" arrows each time the ROC rose above, and then fell below, the overbought level of +6.5.

The optimum overbought/oversold levels (e.g., ±6.5) vary, depending on the security being analyzed and overall market conditions. I selected ±6.5 by drawing a horizontal line on the chart that isolated previous "extreme" levels of Walgreen's 12-day ROC.

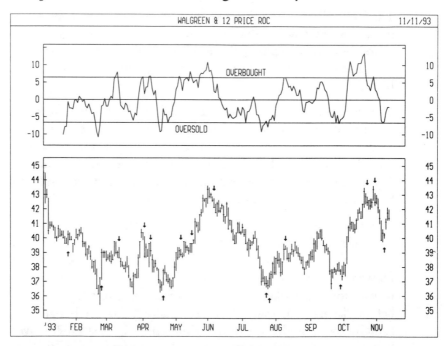

CALCULATION

When the Rate-of-Change displays the price change in points, it subtracts the price x time periods ago from today's price:

Today's Close – Close x-periods ago

When the Rate-of-Change displays the price change as a percentage, it divides the price change by price x time period's ago:

$$\left(\frac{Today's\ Close - Close\ x-periods\ ago}{Close\ x-periods\ ago} \right) * 100$$

PUBLIC SHORT RATIO

OVERVIEW

The Public Short Ratio (PSR) shows the relationship between the number of public short sales and the total number of short sales. (The Public Short Ratio is sometimes referred to as the nonmember short ratio.)

INTERPRETATION

The interpretation of the PSR assumes one premise: that of the short sellers, the public is the worst (well, except for the odd- lot traders, whose indicators begin on page 201). If this is true, then we should buy when the public is shorting and sell when the public is long. Historically, this premise has held true.

Generally speaking, the higher the PSR, the more bearish the public, and the more likely prices will increase (given the above premise). Historically, it has been considered bullish when the 10-week moving average of the PSR is above 25 percent and bearish when the moving average is below 25 percent. The further the moving average is in the bullish or bearish territory, the more likely it is that a correction/rally will take place. Also, the longer the indicator is in the bullish/bearish territory, the better the chances of a market move. For more information on the PSR, I suggest reading the discussion on the nonmember short ratio in *Stock Market Logic*, by Norman G. Fosback.

EXAMPLE

The following chart shows the New York Stock Exchange Index and a 10-week moving average of the Public Short Ratio.

The PSR dropped below 25 percent into bearish territory at the point labeled A. Over the next several months, the PSR continued to move lower as the public became more and more bullish. During this period, prices surged upward, adding to the bullish frenzy. The subsequent crash of 1987 gave the public a strong dose of reality.

Since the crash of 1987, the PSR has remained high, telling us that the public doesn't expect higher prices—a bullish sign.

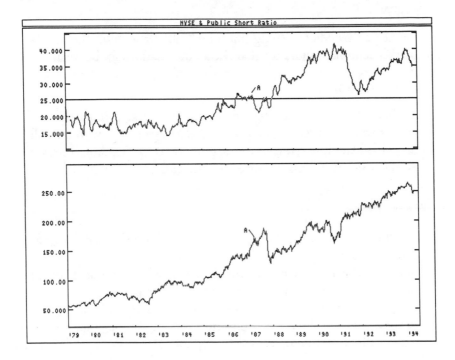

CALCULATION

The Public Short Ratio is calculated by dividing the number of public short sales by the total number of short sales. The result is the percentage of public shorts.

$$\frac{Total\ Public\ Short\ Sales}{Total\ Short\ Sales}$$

PUTS/CALLS RATIO

OVERVIEW

Developed by Martin Zweig, the Puts/Calls Ratio (P/C Ratio) is a market sentiment indicator that shows the relationship between the number of puts to calls traded on the Chicago Board Options Exchange (CBOE).

Traditionally, options are traded by unsophisticated, impatient investors who are lured by the potential for huge profits with a small capital outlay. Interestingly, the actions of these investors provide excellent signals for market tops and bottoms.

INTERPRETATION

A call gives an investor the right to purchase 100 shares of stock at a predetermined price. Investors who purchase calls expect stock prices to rise in the coming months. Conversely, a put gives an investor the right to sell 100 shares of stock at a pre-set price. Investors purchasing puts expect stock prices to decline. (An exception to these general rules is that puts and calls can also be purchased to hedge other investments, even other options.)

Because investors who purchase calls expect the market to rise, and investors who purchase puts expect the market to decline, the relationship between the number of puts and calls illustrates the bullish/bearish expectations of these traditionally ineffective investors.

The higher the level of the P/C Ratio, the more bearish these investors are on the market. Conversely, lower readings indicate high call volume and thus bullish expectations.

The P/C Ratio is a contrarian indicator. When it reaches "excessive" levels, the market usually corrects by moving in the opposite direction. Table 12 defines general guidelines for interpreting the P/C Ratio. However, the market does not have to correct itself just because investors are excessive in their bullish/bearish beliefs! As with all technical analysis tools, you should use the P/C Ratio in conjunction with other market indicators.

TABLE 12

	P/C RATIO 10-DAY MOVING AVERAGE	P/C RATIO 4-WEEK MOVING AVERAGE
Excessively Bearish (buy)	greater than 80	greater than 70
Excessively Bullish (sell)	less than 45	less than 40

EXAMPLE

The following chart shows the S&P 500 and a four-week moving average of the Puts/Calls Ratio. I drew "buy" arrows when investors were excessively pessimistic (greater than 70) and "sell" arrows when they were excessively optimistic (less than 40). The arrows certainly show that investors are buying puts when they should be buying calls, and vice versa.

CALCULATION

The Puts/Calls Ratio is calculated by dividing the volume of puts by the volume of calls.

$$\frac{Total\ CBOE\ Put\ Volume}{Total\ CBOE\ Call\ Volume}$$

QUADRANT LINES

OVERVIEW

Quadrant Lines are a series of horizontal lines that divide the highest and lowest values (usually prices) into four equal sections.

INTERPRETATION

Quadrant Lines are primarily intended to aid in the visual inspection of price movements. They help you see the highest, lowest, and average price during a specified period.

EXAMPLE

An interesting technique is to display a Linear Regression trendline (see page 163) and Quadrant Lines. This combination displays the highest, lowest, and average price, as well as the average slope of the prices. I used this technique on the following chart of Black & Decker.

CALCULATION

Quadrant Lines are calculated by finding the highest-high and the lowest-low during the time period being analyzed. The top line is drawn at the highest price during the time period, and the bottom line is drawn at the lowest price during the time period. The remaining three lines are then drawn so that they divide the section between the highest-high and the lowest-low into four equal sections. The center line (the "mean") is usually displayed as a dotted line.

RELATIVE STRENGTH, COMPARATIVE

OVERVIEW

Comparative Relative Strength compares two securities to show how the securities are performing relative to each other. Be careful not to confuse Comparative Relative Strength with the Relative Strength Index (see page 255).

INTERPRETATION

Comparative Relative Strength compares a security's price change with that of a "base" security. When the Comparative Relative Strength indicator is moving up, it shows that the security is performing better than the base security. When the indicator is moving sideways, it shows that both securities are performing the same (i.e., rising and falling by the same percentages). When the indicator is moving down, it shows that the security is performing worse than the base security (i.e., not rising as fast or falling faster).

Comparative Relative Strength is often used to compare a security's performance with a market index. It is also useful in developing spreads (i.e., buy the best performer and short the weaker issue).

EXAMPLE

In the following illustration, the top chart displays both Microsoft's and IBM's prices. The bottom chart shows the Comparative Relative Strength of IBM compared to Microsoft.

The Comparative Relative Strength indicator shows that IBM's price outperformed Microsoft's price during the last three months of 1993. It also shows that IBM's price then underperformed Microsoft's price during the first three months of 1994. (I drew the trendlines on the Comparative Relative Strength indicator using the Linear Regression technique, page 163.)

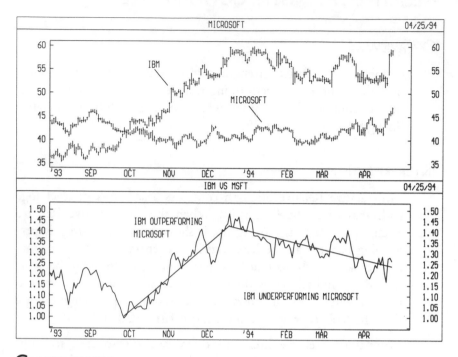

CALCULATION

The Comparative Relative Strength indicator is calculated by dividing one security's price by a second security's price (the "base" security). The result of this division is the ratio, or relationship, between the two securities.

RELATIVE STRENGTH INDEX

OVERVIEW

The Relative Strength Index (RSI) is a popular oscillator. It was first introduced by Welles Wilder in an article in *Commodities* (now known as *Futures*) magazine in June 1978. Step-by-step instructions on calculating and interpreting the RSI are also provided in Mr. Wilder's book, *New Concepts in Technical Trading Systems*.

The name "Relative Strength Index" is slightly misleading, as the RSI does not compare the relative strength of two securities but rather the internal strength of a single security. A more appropriate name might be "Internal Strength Index." Relative strength charts that compare two market indices, which are often referred to as Comparative Relative Strength, are discussed beginning on page 253.

INTERPRETATION

When Wilder introduced the RSI, he recommended using a 14-day RSI. Since then, the 9-day and 25-day RSIs have also gained popularity. Because you can vary the number of time periods in the RSI calculation, I suggest that you experiment to find the period that works best for you. (The fewer days used to calculate the RSI, the more volatile the indicator.)

The RSI is a price-following oscillator that ranges between 0 and 100. A popular method of analyzing the RSI is to look for a divergence (see page 35) in which the security is making a new high, but the RSI is failing to surpass its previous high. This divergence is an indication of an impending reversal. When the RSI then turns down and falls below its most recent trough, it is said to have completed a "failure swing." The failure swing is considered a confirmation of the impending reversal.

In Mr. Wilder's book, he discusses five uses of the RSI in analyzing commodity charts. These methods can be applied to other security types as well.

- **Tops and Bottoms.** The RSI usually tops above 70 and bottoms below 30. It usually forms these tops and bottoms before the underlying price chart.

- **Chart Formations.** The RSI often forms chart patterns such as head-and-shoulders (see page 224) or triangles (see page 226) that may or may not be visible on the price chart.

- **Failure Swings** (also known as support or resistance penetrations or breakouts). This is where the RSI surpasses a previous high (peak) or falls below a recent low (trough).

- **Support and Resistance.** The RSI shows, sometimes more clearly than prices themselves, levels of support and resistance.

- **Divergences.** As discussed above, divergences occur when the price makes a new high (or low) that is not confirmed by a new high (or low) in the RSI. Prices usually correct and move in the direction of the RSI.

For additional information on the RSI, refer to Mr. Wilder's book.

EXAMPLE

The following chart shows PepsiCo and its 14-day RSI. A bullish divergence occurred during May and June as prices were falling while the RSI was rising. Prices subsequently corrected and trended upward.

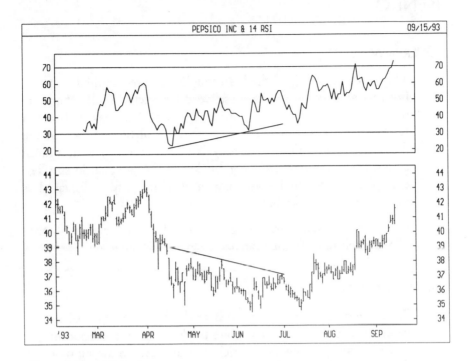

CALCULATION

The RSI is a fairly simple formula, but it is difficult to explain without pages of examples. Refer to Wilder's book for additional calculation information. The basic formula is:

$$100 - \left(\frac{100}{1 + \left(\dfrac{U}{D} \right)} \right)$$

Where:

U = An average of upward price change

D = An average of downward price change

Renko

Overview

The Renko charting method is thought to have acquired its name from *renga*, which is the Japanese word for bricks. Renko charts are similar to Three Line Break charts (see page 275) except that in a Renko chart, a line (or "brick" as they're called) is drawn in the direction of the prior move only if prices move by a minimum amount (i.e., the box size). The bricks are always equal in size. For example, in a 5-unit Renko chart, a 20-point rally is displayed as four 5-unit-tall Renko bricks.

Renko charts were first brought to the United States by Steven Nison when he published the book *Beyond Candlesticks*.

Interpretation

Basic trend reversals are signaled with the emergence of a new white or black brick. A new white brick indicates the beginning of a new uptrend. A new black brick indicates the beginning of a new downtrend. Since the Renko chart is a trend-following technique, there are times when Renko charts produce whipsaws, giving signals near the end of short-lived trends. However, the expectation with a trend-following technique is that it allows you to ride the major portion of significant trends.

Since a Renko chart isolates the underlying price trend by filtering out the minor price changes, Renko charts can also be very helpful when determining support and resistance levels.

Example

The following charts show Intel as a classic high-low-close bar chart and as a 2.5-unit Renko chart. I drew "buy" and "sell" arrows on both charts when trend reversals occurred in the Renko chart. You can see that although the signals were late, they did ensure that you invested with the major trend.

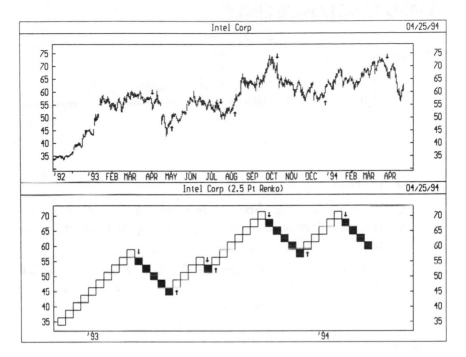

CALCULATION

Renko charts are always based on closing prices. You specify a "box size," which determines the minimum price change to display.

In drawing Renko bricks, today's close is compared with the high and low of the previous brick (white or black):

- If the closing price rises above the top of the previous brick by at least the box size, one or more white bricks are drawn in new columns. The height of the bricks is always equal to the box size.

- If the closing price falls below the bottom of the previous brick by at least the box size, one or more black bricks are drawn in new columns. Again, the height of the bricks is always equal to the box size.

If prices move more than the box size, but not enough to create two bricks, only one brick is drawn. For example, in a two-unit Renko chart, if the prices move from 100 to 103, only one white brick is drawn, from 100 to 102. The rest of the move, from 102 to 103, is not shown on the Renko chart.

Speed resistance lines

Overview

Speed Resistance Lines (SRL), sometimes called 1/3-2/3 lines, are a series of trendlines that divide a price move into three equal sections. They are similar in construction and interpretation to Fibonacci Fan Lines (see page 135).

Interpretation

Speed Resistance Lines display three trendlines. The slope of each line defines a different rate at which pricing expectations are changing.

Prices should find support above the 2/3 line. When prices do fall below the 2/3 line, they should quickly drop to the 1/3 line, where they should then again find support.

Example

The following charts show McDonald's price and Speed Resistance Lines. The initial trendline was drawn from the low point, labeled A, to the high point, labeled B. You can see that prices found support each time they fell to the 2/3 line. When prices finally penetrated the 2/3 line (at point C) they quickly fell to the 1/3 line, where they again found support.

Calculation

To draw Speed Resistance Lines:

1. Draw a line from a major low to a major high.

2. Draw a vertical line on the day the major high occurred. Divide this vertical line into thirds.

3. Draw lines from the major low so that they intersect the vertical line at the 1/3 and 2/3 levels.

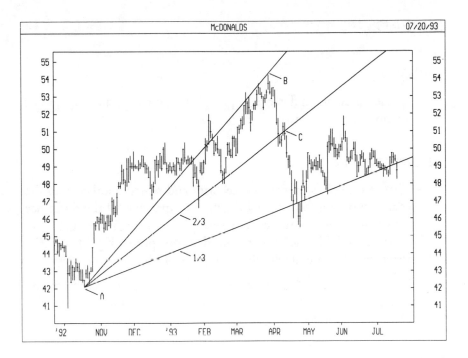

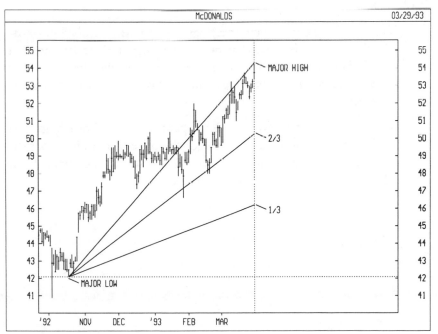

SPREADS

OVERVIEW

Spreads show the difference in price between two securities. Spreads are normally calculated using options.

INTERPRETATION

A spread involves buying one security and selling another with the goal of profiting from the narrowing or expanding of the difference between the two securities. For example, you might buy gold and short silver with the expectation that the price of gold will rise faster (or fall more slowly) than the price of silver.

You can also spread a single security by buying one contract and selling another. For example, buy an October contract and sell a December contract.

EXAMPLE

The following charts show live hogs (top chart), pork bellies (middle chart), and the spread between the hogs and bellies (bottom chart). This spread involves buying the hogs and shorting the bellies with the anticipation that hogs will rise faster (or fall more slowly) than bellies.

You can see that during the time period shown, both hogs and bellies decreased in price. As desired, the price of hogs fell less than the price of bellies. This is shown by the spread narrowing from −10.55 to −3.58, with a resulting profit of 6.97.

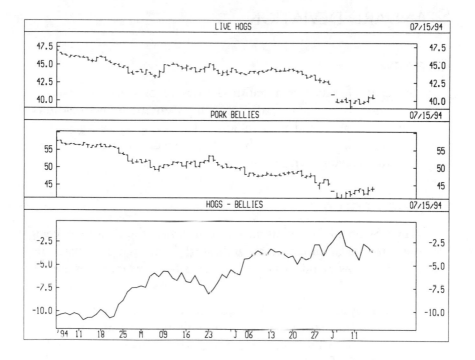

STANDARD DEVIATION

OVERVIEW

Standard Deviation is a statistical measure of volatility. Standard Deviation is typically used as a component of other indicators, rather than as a stand-alone indicator. For example, Bollinger Bands (see page 72) are calculated by adding a security's Standard Deviation to a moving average.

INTERPRETATION

High Standard Deviation values occur when the data item being analyzed (e.g., prices or an indicator) is changing dramatically. Similarly, low Standard Deviation values occur when prices are stable.

Many analysts feel that major tops are accompanied by high volatility as investors struggle with both euphoria and fear. Major bottoms are expected to be calmer, since investors have few expectations of profits.

EXAMPLE

The following chart shows Procter & Gamble and its 10-week Standard Deviation. The extremely low Standard Deviation values at points A and B preceded significant rallies at points 1 and 2.

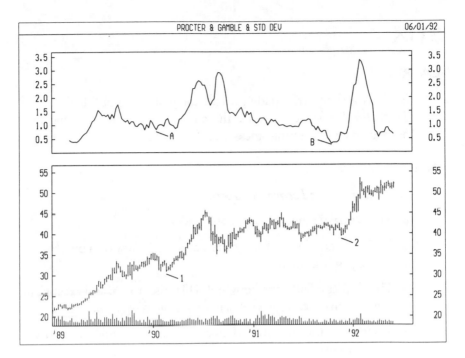

CALCULATION

$$\sqrt{\dfrac{\sum\limits_{j=1}^{n}\left(Close_j \ - \ n\text{-period SMA of Close}\right)^2}{n}}$$

Where:

SMA = Simple Moving Average

n = Number of time periods

Standard Deviation is derived by calculating an n-period simple moving average of the data item (i.e., the closing price or an indicator), summing the squares of the difference between the data item and its moving average over each of the preceding n time periods, dividing this sum by n, and then calculating the square root of this result.

STIX

OVERVIEW

STIX is a short-term trading oscillator that was published in *The Polymetric Report*. It compares the amount of volume flowing into advancing and declining stocks.

INTERPRETATION

According to *The Polymetric Report:*

- STIX usually ranges between +42 and +58.

- If STIX gets as low as 45, the market is almost always a buy, except in a raging bear market.

- The market is fairly overbought if STIX rises to 56; and except in a new bull market, it's wise to sell if STIX goes over 58.

- Traders and investors should modify these rough rules to suit their own objectives.

- In normal markets, STIX rarely gets as high as 56 or as low as 45, so rigid use of these rules of thumb would keep you inactive most of the time. For active accounts, the rules might be made much less stringent (see Table 13).

TABLE 13

Extremely Overbought	greater than 58
Fairly Overbought	greater than 56
Fairly Oversold	less than 45
Extremely Oversold	less than 42

EXAMPLE

The following chart shows the S&P 500 and the STIX indicator. I drew "buy" arrows when the STIX fell below, and then rose above, the oversold level of 45. I drew "sell" arrows when the STIX rose above, and then fell below, the overbought level of 56.

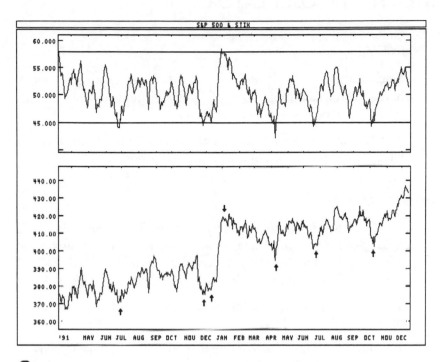

CALCULATION

STIX is based on a variation of the Advance/Decline Ratio (see page 59):

$$A/D \; Ratio = \left(\frac{Advancing \;\; Issues}{Advancing \;\; Issues + Declining \;\; Issues} \right) * 100$$

The STIX is a 21-period (i.e., 9 percent) exponential moving average of the above A/D Ratio:

$$STIX = (A/D \; Ratio * 0.09) + (Yesterday's \; STIX * 0.91)$$

Stochastic oscillator

Overview

Stochastic (stō kas′ tik) *adj.* . . . 2. *Math.* designating a process having an infinite progression of jointly distributed random variables. —*Webster's New World Dictionary*

The Stochastic Oscillator compares where a security's price closed relative to its price range over a given time period.

Interpretation

The Stochastic Oscillator is displayed as two lines. The main line is called %K. The second line, called %D, is a moving average of %K. The %K line is usually displayed as a solid line, and the %D line is usually displayed as a dotted line.

There are several ways to interpret a Stochastic Oscillator. Three popular methods include:

1. Buy when the Oscillator (either %K or %D) falls below a specific level (e.g., 20) and then rises above that level. Sell when the Oscillator rises above a specific level (e.g., 80) and then falls below that level.

2. Buy when the %K line rises above the %D line and sell when the %K line falls below the %D line.

3. Look for divergences (see page 35), for example, where prices are making a series of new highs and the Stochastic Oscillator is failing to surpass its previous highs.

Example

The following chart shows California Energy and its 10-day Stochastic. I drew "buy" arrows when the %K line fell below, and then rose above, the level of 20. Similarly, I drew "sell" arrows when the %K line rose above, and then fell below, the level of 80.

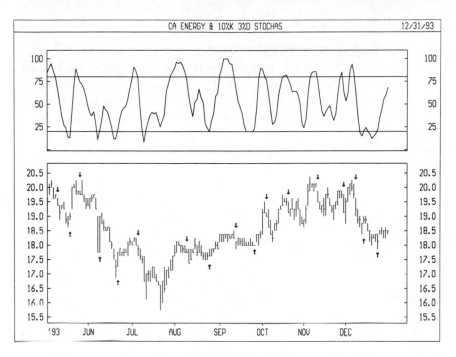

This next chart also shows California Energy. In this example I drew "buy" arrows each time the %K line rose above the %D (dotted). Similarly, "sell" arrows were drawn when the %K line fell below the %D line.

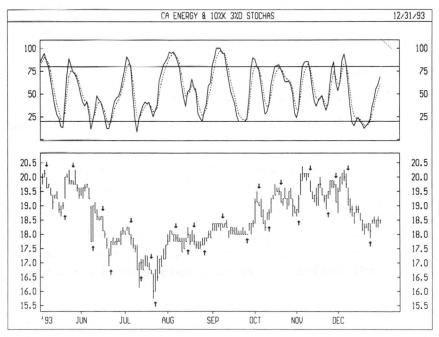

This final chart shows a divergence between the Stochastic Oscillator and prices. This is a classic divergence where prices are headed higher but the underlying indicator (the Stochastic Oscillator) is moving lower. When a divergence occurs between an indicator and prices, the indicator typically provides the clue as to where prices will head.

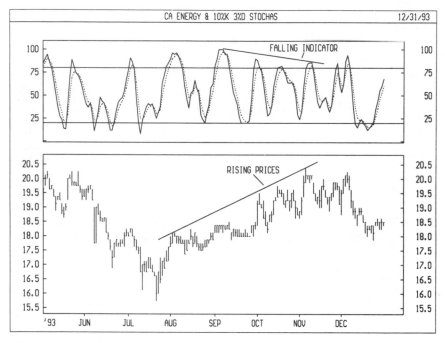

CALCULATION

The Stochastic Oscillator has four variables:

1. **%K Periods.** This is the number of time periods used in the stochastic calculation.

2. **%K Slowing Periods.** This value controls the internal smoothing of %K. A value of 1 is considered a fast stochastic; a value of 3 is considered a slow stochastic.

3. **%D Periods.** This is the number of time periods used when calculating a moving average of %K. The moving average is called %D and is usually displayed as a dotted line on top of %K.

4. **%D Method.** The method (i.e., Exponential, Simple, Time Series, Triangular, Variable, or Weighted) that is used to calculate %D.

The formula for %K is:

$$\left(\frac{Today's\ Close\ -\ Lowest\ Low\ in\ \%K\ Periods}{Highest\ High\ in\ \%K\ Periods\ -\ Lowest\ Low\ in\ \%K\ Periods} \right) * 100$$

For example, to calculate a 10-day %K, first find the security's highest-high and lowest-low over the last 10 days. As an example, let's assume that during the last 10 days the highest-high was 46 and the lowest-low was 38—a range of 8 points. If today's closing price was 41, %K would be calculated as:

$$37.5 = \left(\frac{41\ -\ 38}{46\ -\ 38} \right) * 100$$

The 37.5 percent in this example shows that today's close was at the level of 37.5 percent relative to the security's trading range over the last 10 days. If today's close was 42, the Stochastic Oscillator would be 50 percent. This would mean that the security closed today at 50 percent, or the midpoint, of its 10-day trading range.

The above example used a %K Slowing Period of 1 day (no slowing). If you use a value greater than 1, you average the highest-high and the lowest-low over the number of %K Slowing Periods before performing the division.

A moving average of %K is then calculated using the number of time periods specified in the %D Periods. This moving average is called %D.

The Stochastic Oscillator always ranges between 0 percent and 100 percent. A reading of 0 percent shows that the security's close was the lowest price that the security has traded during the preceding x time periods. A reading of 100 percent shows that the security's close was the highest price that the security has traded during the preceding x time periods.

SWING INDEX

OVERVIEW

Developed by Welles Wilder, the Swing Index seeks to isolate the "real" price of a security by comparing the relationships between the current prices (i.e., open, high, low, and close) and the previous period's prices.

INTERPRETATION

The Swing Index is primarily used as a component of the *Accumulation* Swing Index (see page 54).

EXAMPLE

The following chart shows the British pound and the Swing Index. You can see that by itself, the Swing Index is an erratic plot. The value of this indicator develops when it is accumulated into the Accumulation Swing Index (see page 54).

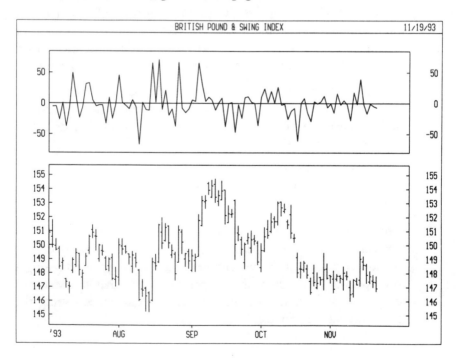

CALCULATION

Although it is beyond the scope of this book to completely define the Swing Index, the basic formula is shown below. Step-by-step instructions on calculating the Swing Index are provided in Wilder's book, *New Concepts In Technical Trading Systems*.

$$50 * \left(\frac{C - Cy + 0.5(C - O) + 0.25\ (Cy - Oy)}{R} \right) * \frac{K}{T}$$

Where:

C	=	Today's closing price
Cy	=	Yesterday's closing price
Hy	=	Yesterday's highest price
K	■	The largest of: Hy-C and Ly-C
L	=	Today's lowest price
Ly	=	Yesterday's lowest price
O	=	Today's opening price
Oy	=	Yesterday's opening price
R	=	A complex calculation based on the relationship between today's closing price and yesterday's high and low prices.
T	=	The value of a limit move (see the table that follows)

Table 14 lists the limit moves for several commodities. You can get a list of limit moves from your broker.

TABLE 14

COMMODITY	LIMIT MOVE
Coffee	$0.06
Gold	$75.00
Heating Oil	$0.04
Hogs	$0.015
Soybeans	$0.30
T-Bonds	$3.00

You may need to adjust the limit moves shown in Table 14, based on the position of the decimal in your data. For example, if the price of corn is quoted as $2.45, the limit move would be $0.10. However, if the price of corn is quoted as $245.00, the limit move would be $10.00.

If the security does not have a limit move (e.g., a stock or some futures), use an extremely high value (e.g., $30,000).

THREE LINE BREAK

OVERVIEW

Three Line Break charts display a series of vertical boxes ("lines") that are based on changes in prices. As with Kagi (see page 158), Point and Figure (see page 233), and Renko charts (see page 258), Three Line Break charts ignore the passage of time.

The Three Line Break charting method is so named because of the number of lines typically used.

Three Line Break charts were first brought to the United States by Steven Nison when he published the book *Beyond Candlesticks.*

INTERPRETATION

The following are the basic trading rules for a Three Line Break chart:

- Buy when a white line emerges after three adjacent black lines (a "white turnaround line").

- Sell when a black line appears after three adjacent white lines (a "black turnaround line").

- Avoid trading in "trendless" markets where the lines alternate between black and white.

An advantage of Three Line Break charts is that there is no arbitrary fixed reversal amount. It is the price action that gives the indication of a reversal. The disadvantage of Three Line Break charts is that the signals are generated after the new trend is well under way. However, many traders are willing to accept the late signals in exchange for calling major trends.

You can adjust the sensitivity of the reversal criteria by changing the number of lines in the break. For example, short-term traders might use two-line breaks to get more reversals, while a longer-term investor might use four-line or even 10-line breaks to reduce the number of reversals. The Three Line Break is the most popular in Japan.

Steven Nison recommends using Three Line Break charts in conjunction with candlestick charts (see page 79). He suggests using the Three Line Break chart to determine the prevailing trend and then using candlestick patterns to time your individual trades.

EXAMPLE

The following illustration shows a Three Line Break and a bar chart of Apple Computer. You can see that the number of break lines in a given month depends on the price change during the month. For example, June has many lines because the prices changed significantly, whereas November has only two lines because prices were relatively flat.

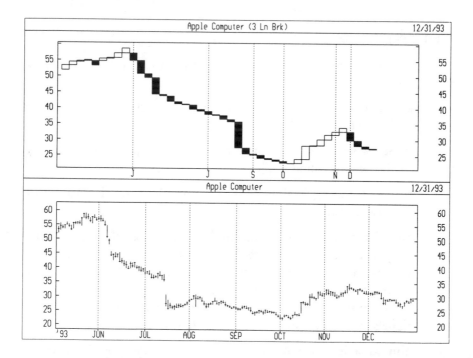

CALCULATION

Line Break charts are always based on closing prices. The general rules for calculating a Line Break chart are:

- If the price exceeds the previous line's high price, a new white line is drawn.

- If the price falls below the previous line's low price, a new black line is drawn.

- If the price does not rise above nor fall below the previous line, nothing is drawn.

In a Three Line Break chart, if rallies are strong enough to display three consecutive lines of the same color, then prices must reverse by the extreme price of the last three lines in order to create a new line:

- If a rally is powerful enough to form three consecutive *white* lines, then prices must fall below the lowest point of the last three white lines before a new black line is drawn.

- If a sell-off is powerful enough to form three consecutive *black* lines, then prices must rise above the highest point of the last three black lines before a new white line is drawn.

TIME SERIES FORECAST

OVERVIEW

The Time Series Forecast indicator displays the statistical trend of a security's price over a specified time period. The trend is based on linear regression analysis. Rather than plotting a straight linear regression trendline (see page 163), the Time Series Forecast plots the last point of multiple linear regression trendlines. The resulting Time Series Forecast indicator is sometimes referred to as the "moving linear regression" indicator or the "regression oscillator."

INTERPRETATION

The interpretation of a Time Series Forecast is identical to a moving average. However, the Time Series Forecast indicator has two advantages over classic moving averages.

Unlike a moving average, a Time Series Forecast does not exhibit as much delay when adjusting to price changes. Since the indicator is "fitting" itself to the data rather than averaging them, the Time Series Forecast is more responsive to price changes.

As the name suggests, you can use the Time Series Forecast to forecast the next period's price. This estimate is based on the trend of the security's prices over the period specified (e.g., 20 days). If the current trend continues, the value of the Time Series Forecast is a forecast of the next period's price.

EXAMPLE

The following chart shows a 50-day Time Series Forecast of Microsoft's prices. I've also drawn three 50-day-long linear regression trendlines. You can see that the ending point of each trendline is equal to the value of the Time Series Forecast.

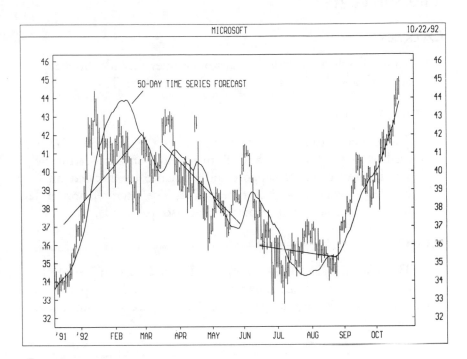

50-DAY TIME SERIES FORECAST

CALCULATION

The Time Series Forecast is determined by calculating a linear regression trendline using the "least squares fit" method. The least squares fit technique fits a trendline to the data in the chart by minimizing the distance between the data points and the linear regression trendline. The formula for a linear regression trendline is given on page 164.

TIRONE LEVELS

OVERVIEW

Tirone Levels are a series of horizontal lines that identify support and resistance levels. They were developed by John Tirone.

INTERPRETATION

Tirone Levels can be drawn using either the Midpoint 1/3-2/3 method or the Mean method. Both methods are intended to help you identify potential support and resistance levels based on the range of prices over a given time period. The interpretation of Tirone Levels is similar to Quadrant Lines (see page 251).

EXAMPLE

The following chart shows Midpoint Tirone Levels on Lincoln National. The dotted line shows the average price. The top and bottom lines divide the range between the highest and lowest prices into thirds.

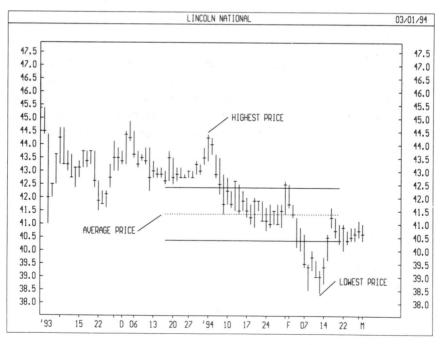

CALCULATION

MIDPOINT METHOD

Midpoint levels are calculated by finding the highest-high and the lowest-low during the time period being analyzed. The lines are then calculated as follows:

- **Top line:** Subtract the lowest-low from the highest-high, divide this value by three, and then subtract this result from the highest-high.

- **Center Line:** Subtract the lowest-low from the highest-high, divide this value by two, and then add this result to the lowest-low.

- **Bottom Line:** Subtract the lowest-low from the highest-high, divide this value by three, and then add this result to the lowest-low.

MEAN METHOD

Mean levels are displayed as five lines (the spacing between the lines is not necessarily symmetrical). The lines are calculated as follows:

- **Extreme High:** Subtract the lowest-low from the highest-high and add this value to the Adjusted Mean.

- **Regular High:** Subtract the lowest-low from the value of the Adjusted Mean multiplied by two.

- **Adjusted Mean:** This is the sum of the highest-high, the lowest-low, and the most recent closing price, divided by three.

- **Regular Low:** Subtract the highest-high from the value of the Adjusted Mean multiplied by two.

- **Extreme Low:** Subtract the lowest-low from the highest-high and then subtract this value from the Adjusted Mean.

TOTAL SHORT RATIO

OVERVIEW

The Total Short Ratio (TSR) shows the percentage of short sales to the total volume on the New York Stock Exchange.

INTERPRETATION

As with the Public Short Ratio, the Total Short Ratio takes the contrarian view that short sellers are usually wrong. While the odd lotters are typically the worst of the short sellers, history has shown that even the specialists tend to over-short at market bottoms.

The TSR shows investor expectations. High values indicate bearish expectations and low values indicate bullish expectations. Taking a contrarian stance, when there are high levels of shorts (many investors expect a market decline), we would expect the market to rise. Likewise, extremely low levels of short sales should indicate excessive optimism and the increased likelihood of a market decline.

The interpretation of all of the short sale indicators has become more difficult recently due to option hedging and arbitrage. However, they are still helpful in determining overall market expectations.

EXAMPLE

The following chart shows the New York Stock Exchange and a 10-week moving average of the Total Short Ratio. I drew "buy" arrows each time investors were excessively bearish. In hindsight, each of these turned out to be excellent times to enter the market.

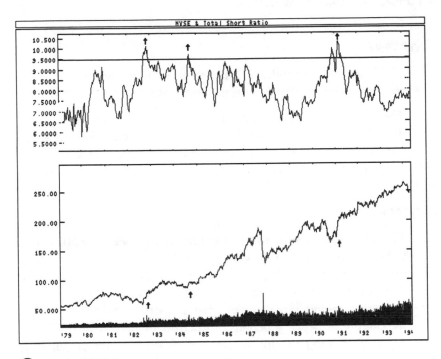

CALCULATION

The Total Short Ratio is calculated by dividing the total number of short sales by the total number of buy and sell orders. Both of these figures are reported weekly (on Fridays) by the NYSE.

$$\left(\frac{Total\ Short\ Sales}{Total\ Buy/Sell\ Orders} \right) * 100$$

TRADE VOLUME INDEX

OVERVIEW

The Trade Volume Index (TVI) shows whether a security is being accumulated (purchased) or distributed (sold).

The TVI is designed to be calculated using intraday "tick" price data. The TVI is based on the premise that trades taking place at higher "asking" prices are buy transactions and trades at lower "bid" prices are sell transactions.

INTERPRETATION

The TVI is very similar to On Balance Volume (see page 207). The OBV method works well with daily prices, but it doesn't work as well with intraday tick prices. Tick prices, especially stock prices, often display trades at the bid or ask price for extended periods without changing. This creates a flat support or resistance level in the chart. During these periods of unchanging prices, the TVI continues to accumulate this volume on either the buy or sell side, depending on the last price change.

The TVI helps identify whether a security is being accumulated or distributed. When the TVI is trending up, it shows that trades are taking place at the asking price as buyers accumulate the security. When the TVI is trending down, it shows that trades are taking place at the bid price as sellers distribute the security.

When prices create a flat resistance level and the TVI is rising, look for prices to breakout to the upside. When prices create a flat support level and the TVI is falling, look for prices to drop below the support level.

EXAMPLE

The following chart shows IBM's tick prices and TVI. During the 45 minutes leading up to the point labeled A, prices were locked in a tight range between the bid price of 69 1/4 and the asking price of 69 3/8. During this same period, the TVI was trending upward, which showed that the prices were slowly being accumulated.

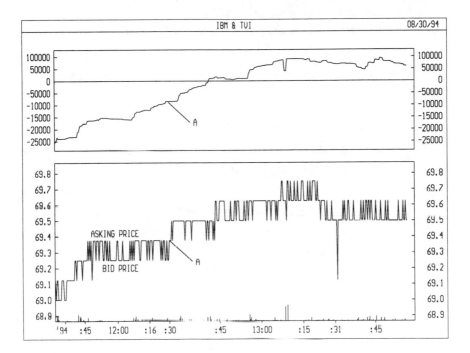

CALCULATION

The Trade Volume Index is calculated by adding each trade's volume to a cumulative total when the price moves up by a specified amount, and subtracting the trade's volume when the price moves down by a specified amount. The "specified" amount is called the Minimum Tick Value.

To calculate the TVI you must first determine if prices are being accumulated or distributed:

Change = Price − Last Price
MTV = Minimum Tick Value

If Change is greater than MTV, then
    Direction = Accumulate

If Change is less than −MTV, then
Direction = Distribute

If Change is less than or equal to MTV and
Change is greater than or equal to −MTV, then
Direction = Last Direction

Once you know the direction, you can then calculate the TVI:

If Direction is Accumulate, then
TVI = TVI + Today's Volume

If Direction is Distribute, then
TVI = TVI − Today's Volume

TRENDLINES

OVERVIEW

One of the basic tenets put forth by Charles Dow in the Dow Theory is that security prices do trend. Trends are often measured and identified by "trendlines." A trendline is a sloping line that is drawn between two or more prominent points on a chart. Rising trends are defined by a trendline that is drawn between two or more troughs (low points) to identify price support. Falling trends are defined by trendlines that are drawn between two or more peaks (high points) to identify price resistance.

INTERPRETATION

A principle of technical analysis is that once a trend has been formed (two or more peaks/troughs have touched the trendline and reversed direction) it will remain intact until broken.

That sounds much more simplistic than it is! The goal is to analyze the current trend using trendlines and then either invest with the current trend until the trendline is broken, or wait for the trendline to be broken and then invest with the new (opposite) trend.

One benefit of trendlines is that they help distinguish emotional decisions ("I think it's time to sell...") from analytical decisions ("I will hold until the current rising trendline is broken"). Another benefit of trendlines is that they almost always keep you on the "right" side of the market. When using trendlines, it's difficult to hold a security for very long when prices are falling just as it's hard to be short when prices are rising— either way the trendline will be broken.

EXAMPLE

The following chart shows Goodyear along with several trendlines. Trendlines A and C are falling trendlines. Note how they were drawn between successive peaks. Trendlines B and D are rising trendlines. They were drawn between successive troughs in the price.

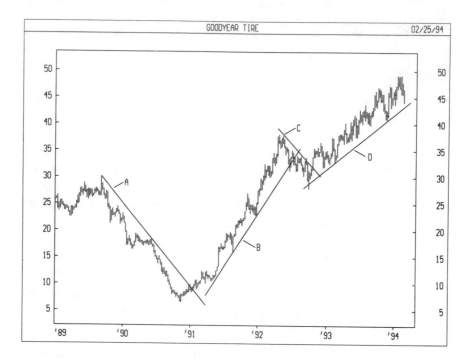

GOODYEAR TIRE — 02/25/94

TRIX

OVERVIEW

TRIX is a momentum indicator that displays the percent rate-of-change of a triple exponentially smoothed moving average of the security's closing price. It is designed to keep you in trends equal to or shorter than the number of periods you specify.

INTERPRETATION

The TRIX indicator oscillates around a zero line. Its triple exponential smoothing is designed to filter out "insignificant" cycles (i.e., those that are shorter than the number of periods you specify).

Trades should be placed when the indicator changes direction (i.e., buy when it turns up and sell when it turns down). You may want to plot a nine-period moving average of the TRIX to create a "signal" line (similar to the MACD indicator, page 166), and then buy when the TRIX rises above its signal and sell when it falls below its signal.

Divergences between the security and the TRIX can also help identify turning points.

EXAMPLE

The following chart shows Checker Drive-In, its 12-day TRIX (solid line), and a 9-day "signal" moving average of the TRIX (dotted line). I drew "buy" arrows when the TRIX rose above its signal line and "sell" arrows when it fell below its signal line. This method worked well when prices were trending, but it generated numerous false signals when prices were moving sideways.

A bearish divergence occurred when the TRIX was falling (trendline A) while prices rose. Prices subsequently corrected. Similarly, a bullish divergence occurred when the TRIX was rising (trendline B) while prices were falling. Prices subsequently rallied.

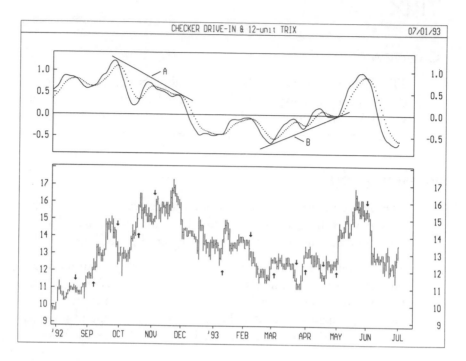

CALCULATION

To calculate the TRIX indicator:

1. Calculate an *n*-period exponential moving average of the closing prices.

2. Calculate an *n*-period exponential moving average of the moving average calculated in Step 1.

3. Calculate an *n*-period exponential moving average of the moving average calculated in Step 2.

4. Calculate the one-period (e.g., one-day) percent change of the moving average calculated in Step 3.

TYPICAL PRICE

OVERVIEW

The Typical Price indicator is simply an average of each day's price. The Median Price (see page 177) and the Weighted Close (see page 312 are similar indicators.

INTERPRETATION

The Typical Price indicator provides a simple, single-line plot of the day's average price. Some investors use the Typical Price rather than the closing price when creating moving average penetration systems.

The Typical Price is a building block of the Money Flow Index (see page 182).

EXAMPLE

The following chart shows the Typical Price indicator on top of Value Line's bar chart.

CALCULATION

The Typical Price indicator is calculated by adding the high, low, and closing prices together, and then dividing by three. The result is the average, or typical price.

$$Typical\ Price = \frac{(High + Low + Close)}{3}$$

ULTIMATE OSCILLATOR

OVERVIEW

Oscillators typically compare a security's smoothed price with its price *x* periods ago. Larry Williams noted that the value of this type of oscillator can vary greatly depending on the number of time periods used during the calculation. Thus, he developed the Ultimate Oscillator, which uses weighted sums of three oscillators, each of which uses a different time period.

The three oscillators are based on Williams' definitions of buying and selling "pressure."

INTERPRETATION

Williams recommends that you initiate a trade following a divergence (see page 35) and a breakout in the Ultimate Oscillator's trend. The following text summarizes these rules.

Buy when:

1. A bullish divergence occurs. This is when the security's price makes a lower-low that is not confirmed by a lower-low in the Oscillator.

2. During the bullish divergence, the Oscillator falls below 30.

3. The Oscillator then rises above the highest point reached during the span of the bullish divergence. This is the point at which you buy.

Close long positions when:

■ The conditions are met to sell short (explained below), or

■ The Oscillator rises above 50 and then falls below 45, or

■ The Oscillator rises above 70. (I sometimes wait for the oscillator to then fall below 70.)

Sell short when:

1. A bearish divergence occurs. This is when the security's price makes a higher-high that is not confirmed by a higher-high in the Oscillator.

2. During the bearish divergence, the Oscillator rises above 50.

3. The Oscillator then falls below the lowest point reached during the span of the bearish divergence. This is the point at which you sell short.

Close short positions when:

- The conditions are met to buy long (explained above), or

- The Oscillator rises above 65, or

- The Oscillator falls below 30. (I will sometimes wait for the oscillator to then rise above 30.)

EXAMPLE

The following chart shows Autozone and its Ultimate Oscillator. I drew "sell" arrows when the conditions for a sell signal were met:

- A bearish divergence occurred (lines A) when prices made a new high that was not confirmed by the Oscillator.

- The Oscillator rose above 50 during the divergence.

- The Oscillator fell below the lowest point reached during the span of the divergence (line B).

Similarly, I drew "buy" arrows when the conditions for a buy signal were met:

- A bullish divergence occurred (lines C). Then prices made a new low that was not confirmed by the Oscillator.

- The Oscillator fell below 30 during the divergence.

- The Oscillator rose above the highest point reached during the span of the divergence (line D).

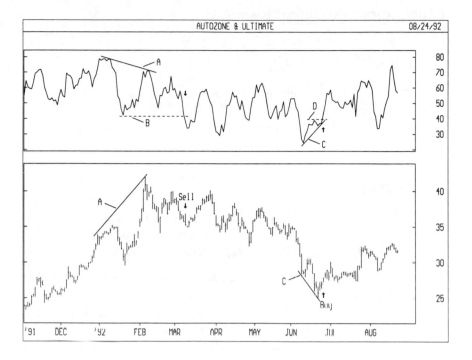

Upside/Downside Ratio

Overview

The Upside/Downside Ratio shows the relationship between up (advancing) and down (declining) volume on the New York Stock Exchange. Advancing, declining, and unchanged volume are discussed on page 63.

Interpretation

When the Upside/Downside Ratio is greater than 1.0, it is showing that there is more volume associated with stocks that are increasing in price than with stocks that are decreasing in price.

While discussing advancing/declining volume in his book *Winning on Wall Street*, Martin Zweig states, "Every bull market in history, and many good intermediate advances, have been launched with a buying stampede that included one or more 9-to-1 days" ("9-to-1" refers to a day were the Upside/Downside Ratio is greater than nine). He goes on to say, "The 9-to-1 up day is a most encouraging sign, and having two of them within a reasonably short span is very bullish. I call it a 'double 9-to-1' when two such days occur within three months of one another."

Table 15 (originally tabulated through 1984 by Martin Zweig) shows all of the double 9-to-1 buy signals that occurred from 1962 to October 1994. As of this writing, no signals have occurred since the last one on June 8, 1988.

Example

The following chart shows the Dow Jones Industrial Average during most of the 1980s. I drew "buy" arrows on the chart where double 9-to-1 buy signals occurred.

TABLE 15

Date	DJIA	% Change 3 months later	% Change 6 months later	% Change 12 months later
11/12/62	624	+8.5	+15.9	+20.2
11/19/63	751	+6.9	+9.1	+16.5
10/12/66	778	+6.9	8.6	+17.4
5/27/70	663	+14.6	+17.8	+16.5
11/19/71	830	+11.8	+17.0	+22.8
9/19/75	830	+1.7	+18.1	+19.9
4/22/80	790	+17.3	+20.9	+27.5
3/22/82	820	−2.4	+13.2	+37.0
8/20/82	869	+15.1	+24.3	+38.4
1/6/83	1,071	+3.9	+14.0	+20.2
8/2/84	1,166	+4.4	+10.6	+16.0
11/23/84	1,220	+4.7	+6.2	+19.3
1/2/87	1,927	+20.4	+26.4	+4.6
10/29/87	1,938	+1.0	+4.9	+10.8
1/4/88	2,015	−1.7	+7.1	+8.0
6/8/88	2,102	−1.9	+1.9	+19.7
AVERAGE		+6.4/qtr.	+12.5/half	+18.4/year

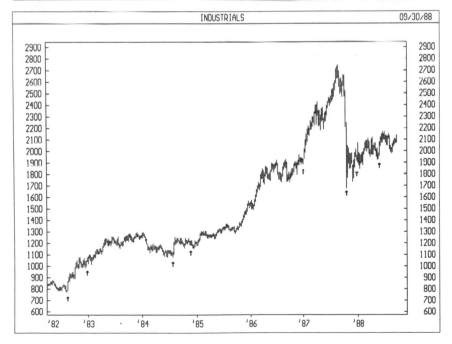

INDUSTRIALS 09/30/88

CALCULATION

The Upside/Downside Ratio is calculated by dividing the daily volume of advancing stocks by the daily volume of declining stocks.

$$\frac{NYSE\ Advancing\ Volume}{NYSE\ Declining\ Volume}$$

UPSIDE-DOWNSIDE VOLUME

OVERVIEW

The Upside-Downside Volume indicator shows the difference between up (advancing) and down (declining) volume on the New York Stock Exchange. Advancing, declining, and unchanged volume are discussed on page 63.

INTERPRETATION

The Upside-Downside Volume indicator shows the net flow of volume into or out of the market. A reading of +40 indicates that up volume exceeded down volume by 40 million shares. Likewise a reading of –40 would indicate that down volume exceeded up volume by 40 million shares.

The indicator is useful to compare today's volume action with previous days. Currently, normal readings are in the area of ±50. Very active days exceed ±150 million shares (the October 1987 crash reached –602).

The Cumulative Volume Index (see page 103) is a cumulative total of the Upside-Downside Volume indicator.

EXAMPLE

The following chart shows the Dow Jones Industrial Average and the Upside-Downside Volume indicator. I labeled the DJIA with "buy" arrows when the Upside-Downside Volume indicator was greater than 200 and with "sell" arrows when the indicator was less than –200.

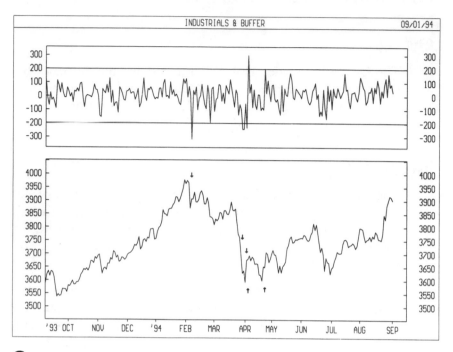

CALCULATION

The Upside-Downside Volume indicator is calculated by subtracting the daily volume of declining stocks from the daily volume of advancing stocks.

NYSE Advancing Volume – NYSE Declining Volume

VERTICAL HORIZONTAL FILTER

OVERVIEW

The Vertical Horizontal Filter (VHF) determines whether prices are in a trending phase or a congestion phase.

The VHF was first presented by Adam White in an article published in the August 1991 issue of *Futures* magazine.

INTERPRETATION

Probably the biggest dilemma in technical analysis is determining if prices are trending or are in a trading range. Trend-following indicators such as the MACD and moving averages are excellent in trending markets, but they usually generate multiple conflicting trades during trading-range (or "congestion") periods. On the other hand, oscillators such as the RSI and Stochastics work well when prices fluctuate within a trading range, but they almost always close positions prematurely during trending markets. The VHF indicator attempts to determine the "trendiness" of prices to help you decide which indicators to use.

There are three ways to interpret the VHF indicator:

1. You can use the VHF values themselves to determine the degree to which prices are trending. The higher the VHF, the higher the degree of trending and the more you should be using trend-following indicators.

2. You can use the direction of the VHF to determine whether a trending or congestion phase is developing. A rising VHF indicates a developing trend; a falling VHF indicates that prices may be entering a congestion phase.

3. You can use the VHF as a contrarian indicator. Expect congestion periods to follow high VHF values; expect prices to trend following low VHF values.

EXAMPLE

The following chart shows Motorola and the VHF indicator. The VHF indicator was relatively low from 1989 through most of 1992. These low values showed that prices were in a trading range. From late 1992 through 1993 the VHF was significantly higher. These higher values indicated that prices were trending.

The 40-week (i.e., 200-day) moving average on Motorola's prices demonstrates the value of the VHF indicator. You can see that a classic moving average trading system (buy when prices rise above their moving average and sell when prices fall below their average) worked well in 1992 and 1993, but generated numerous whipsaws when prices were in a trading range.

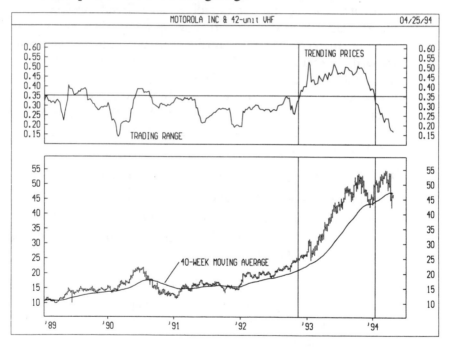

CALCULATION

To calculate the VHF indicator, first determine the highest closing price (HCP) and the lowest closing price (LCP) over the specified time period (often 28-days).

$$HCP = Highest\ closing\ price\ in\ n\ periods$$

$$LCP = Lowest\ closing\ price\ in\ n\ periods$$

Next, subtract the lowest closing price from the highest closing price and take the absolute value of this difference. This value will be the numerator.

$$Numerator = Absolute\ value\ of\ (HCP - LCP)$$

To determine the denominator, sum the absolute value of the difference between each day's price and the previous day's price over the specified time periods.

$$Denominator = \sum_{j=1}^{n} Absolute\ value\ of\ (Close_j - Close_{j-1})$$

The VHF is then calculated by dividing the previously defined numerator by the denominator.

$$VHF = \frac{Numerator}{Denominator}$$

VOLATILITY, CHAIKIN'S

OVERVIEW

Chaikin's Volatility indicator compares the spread between a security's high and low prices. It quantifies volatility as a widening of the range between the high and the low price.

INTERPRETATION

There are two ways to interpret this measure of volatility. One method assumes that market tops are generally accompanied by increased volatility (as investors get nervous and indecisive) and that the latter stages of a market bottom are generally accompanied by decreased volatility (as investors get bored).

Another method (Mr. Chaikin's) assumes that an increase in the Volatility indicator over a relatively short time period indicates that a bottom is near (e.g., a panic sell-off) and that a decrease in volatility over a longer time period indicates an approaching top (e.g., a mature bull market).

As with almost all experienced investors, Mr. Chaikin recommends that you do not rely on any one indicator. He suggests using a moving average penetration or trading band system to confirm this (or any) indicator.

EXAMPLE

The following chart shows the Eurodollar and Chaikin's Volatility indicator. The indicator reached a rapid peak following a panic sell-off (point A). This indicated that a bottom was near (point B).

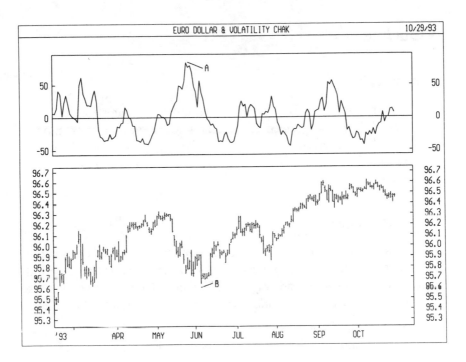

CALCULATION

Chaikin's Volatility is calculated by first calculating an exponential moving average of the difference between the daily high and low prices. Chaikin recommends a 10-day moving average.

H–L Average = Exponential moving average of (High – Low)

Next, calculate the percent that this moving average has changed over a specified time period. Chaikin again recommends 10 days.

$$\left(\frac{(H-L\ Average) - (H-L\ Average\ \ n-periods\ \ ago)}{H-L\ Average\ \ n-periods\ \ ago} \right) * 100$$

VOLUME

OVERVIEW

Volume (see page 7) is simply the number of shares (or contracts) traded during a specified time frame (e.g., hour, day, week, month, etc). The analysis of volume is a basic yet very important element of technical analysis. Volume provides clues as to the intensity of a given price move.

INTERPRETATION

Low volume levels are characteristic of the indecisive expectations that typically occur during consolidation periods (i.e., periods where prices move sideways in a trading range). Low volume also often occurs during the indecisive period during market bottoms.

High volume levels are characteristic of market tops when there is a strong consensus that prices will move higher. High volume levels are also very common at the beginning of new trends (i.e., when prices break out of a trading range). Just before market bottoms, volume will often increase due to panic-driven selling.

Volume can help determine the health of an existing trend. A healthy uptrend should have higher volume on the upward legs of the trend, and lower volume on the downward (corrective) legs. A healthy downtrend usually has higher volume on the downward legs of the trend and lower volume on the upward (corrective) legs.

EXAMPLE

The following chart shows Merck and its volume.

Prices peaked at the end of 1991 following a long rally. This was followed by a price decline (trendline A1). Notice how volume was relatively high during this price decline (trendline A2). The increase in volume during the price decline showed that many investors would sell when prices declined. This was bearish.

Prices then tried to rally (trendline B1). However, volume decreased dramatically (trendline B2) during this rally. This showed that investors were not willing to buy, even when prices were rising. This too, was bearish.

This pattern continued throughout the decline in 1992 and 1993. When prices rallied, they did so on decreased volume. When prices declined, they did so on increased volume. This showed, again and again, that the bears were in control and that prices would continue to fall.

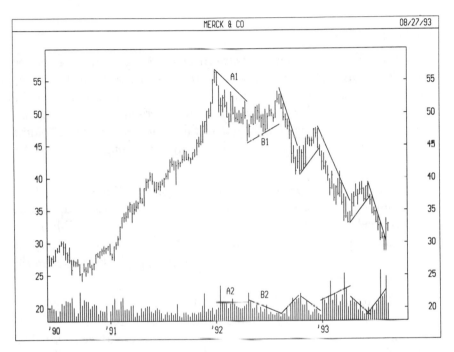

VOLUME OSCILLATOR

OVERVIEW

The Volume Oscillator displays the difference between two moving averages of a security's volume (see page 7). The difference between the moving averages can be expressed in either points or percentages.

INTERPRETATION

You can use the difference between two moving averages of volume to determine if the overall volume trend is increasing or decreasing. When the Volume Oscillator rises above zero, it signifies that the shorter-term volume moving average has risen above the longer-term volume moving average, and thus that the short-term volume trend is higher (i.e., more volume) than the longer-term volume trend.

There are many ways to interpret changes in volume trends. One common belief is that rising prices coupled with increased volume, and falling prices coupled with decreased volume, is bullish. Conversely, if volume increases when prices fall, and volume decreases when prices rise, the market is showing signs of underlying weakness.

The theory behind this is straightforward. Rising prices coupled with increased volume signifies increased upside participation (more buyers) that should lead to a continued move. Conversely, falling prices coupled with increased volume (more sellers) signifies decreased upside participation.

EXAMPLE

The following chart shows Xerox and 5/10-week Volume Oscillator. I drew linear regression trendlines (see page 163) on both the prices and the Volume Oscillator.

This chart shows a healthy pattern. When prices were moving higher, as shown by rising linear regression trendlines, the Volume Oscillator was also rising. When prices were falling, the Volume Oscillator was also falling.

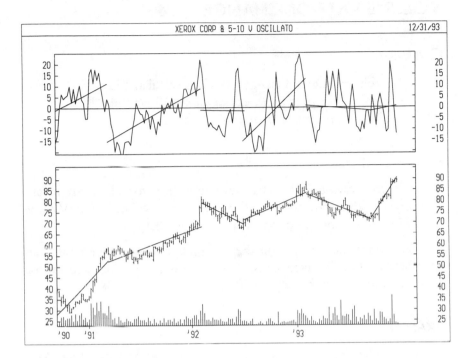

CALCULATION

The Volume Oscillator can display the difference between the two moving averages as either points or percentages. To see the difference in points, subtract the longer-term moving average of volume from the shorter-term moving average of volume:

Shorter Moving Average – Longer Moving Average

To display the difference between the moving averages in percentages, divide the difference between the two moving averages by the shorter-term moving average:

$$\left(\frac{\textit{Shorter Moving Average} - \textit{Longer Moving Average}}{\textit{Shorter Moving Average}}\right) * 100$$

VOLUME RATE-OF-CHANGE

OVERVIEW

The Volume Rate-of-Change (ROC) is calculated identically to the Price ROC (see page 243), except that it displays the ROC of the security's volume rather than of its closing price.

INTERPRETATION

Almost every significant chart formation (e.g., tops, bottoms, break-outs) is accompanied by a sharp increase in volume. The Volume ROC shows the speed at which volume is changing.

Additional information on the interpretation of volume trends can be found in the discussions on Volume (see page 306) and on the Volume Oscillator (see page 308).

EXAMPLE

The following chart shows Texas Instruments and its 12-day Volume ROC. When prices broke out of the triangular pattern, they were accompanied by a sharp increase in volume. The increase in volume confirmed the validity of the price breakout.

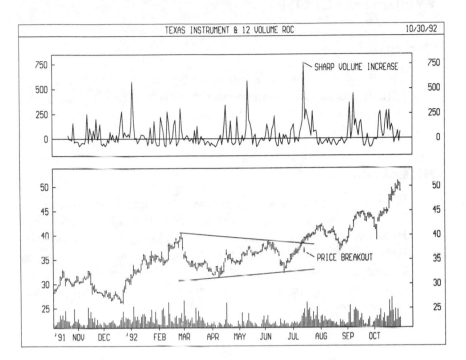

CALCULATION

The Volume Rate-of-Change indicator is calculated by dividing the amount that volume has changed over the last *n* periods by the volume *n* periods ago. The result is the percentage that the volume has changed in the last *n* periods.

If the volume is higher today than *n* periods ago, the ROC will be a positive number. If the volume is lower today than *n* periods ago, the ROC will be a negative number.

$$\left(\frac{Volume \; - \; Volume \; n\text{–}periods \; ago}{Volume \; n\text{–}periods \; ago} \right) * 100$$

WEIGHTED CLOSE

OVERVIEW

The Weighted Close indicator is simply an average of each day's price. It gets its name from the fact that extra weight is given to the closing price. The Median Price (see page 177) and Typical Price (see page 291) are similar indicators.

INTERPRETATION

When plotting and back-testing moving averages, indicators, trendlines, etc., some investors like the simplicity that a line chart offers. However, line charts that show only the closing price can be misleading, since they ignore the high and low price. A Weighted Close chart combines the simplicity of the line chart with the scope of a bar chart, by plotting a single point for each day that includes the high, low, and closing price.

EXAMPLE

The following chart shows the Weighted Close plotted on top of a normal high/low/close bar chart of Peoplesoft.

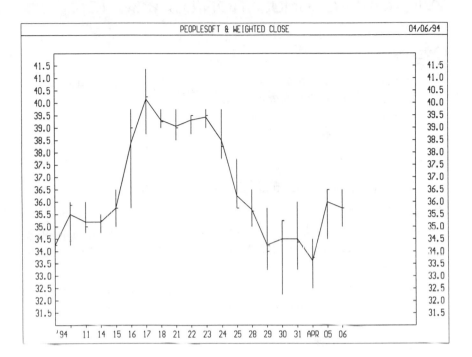

CALCULATION

The Weighted Close indicator is calculated by multiplying the close by two, adding the high and the low to this product, and dividing by four. The result is the average price with extra weight given to the closing price.

$$\frac{(Close * 2) + High + Low}{4}$$

WILLIAMS' ACCUMULATION/DISTRIBUTION

OVERVIEW

Accumulation is a term used to describe a market controlled by buyers, whereas *distribution* is defined by a market controlled by sellers.

INTERPRETATION

Williams recommends trading this indicator based on divergences (see page 35):

- Distribution of the security is indicated when the security is making a new high and the A/D indicator is failing to make a new high. Sell.

- Accumulation of the security is indicated when the security is making a new low and the A/D indicator is failing to make a new low. Buy.

EXAMPLE

The following chart shows Procter & Gamble and the Williams' Accumulation/Distribution indicator. A bearish divergence occurred when the prices were making a new high (point A2) and the A/D indicator was failing to make a new high (point A1). This was the time to sell.

CALCULATION

To calculate Williams' Accumulation/Distribution indicator, first determine the True Range High (TRH) and True Range Low (TRL).

TRH = Yesterday's close or today's high, whichever is greater.

TRL = Yesterday's close or today's low, whichever is less.

Today's accumulation/distribution is then determined by comparing today's closing price to yesterday's closing price.

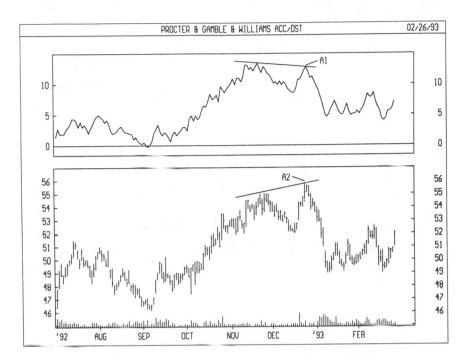

If today's close is greater than yesterday's close:

   Today's A/D = today's close − TRL

If today's close is less than yesterday's close:

   Today's A/D = today's close − TRH

If today's close is equal to yesterday's close:

   Today's A/D = 0

The Williams' Accumulation/Distribution indicator is a cumulative total of these daily values.

   Williams' A/D = Today's A/D + Yesterday's Williams' A/D

WILLIAMS' %R

OVERVIEW

Williams' %R (pronounced "percent R") is a momentum indicator that measures overbought/oversold levels. Williams' %R was developed by Larry Williams.

INTERPRETATION

The interpretation of Williams' %R is very similar to that of the Stochastic Oscillator (see page 268), except that %R is plotted upside-down and the Stochastic Oscillator has internal smoothing.

To display the Williams' %R indicator on an upside-down scale, it is usually plotted using negative values (e.g., -20 percent). For the purpose of analysis and discussion, simply ignore the negative symbols.

Readings in the range of 80 to 100 percent indicate that the security is oversold, while readings in the 0 to 20 percent range suggest that it is overbought.

As with all overbought/oversold indicators, it is best to wait for the security's price to change direction before placing your trades. For example, if an overbought/oversold indicator (such as the Stochastic Oscillator or Williams' %R) is showing an overbought condition, it is wise to wait for the security's price to turn down before selling the security. (The MACD is a good indicator to monitor change in a security's price.) It is not unusual for overbought/oversold indicators to remain in an overbought/oversold condition for a long time period as the security's price continues to climb/fall. Selling simply because the security appears overbought may take you out of the security long before its price shows signs of deterioration.

An interesting phenomenon of the %R indicator is its uncanny ability to anticipate a reversal in the underlying security's price. The indicator almost always forms a peak and turns down a few days before the security's price peaks and turns down. Likewise, %R usually creates a trough and turns up a few days before the security's price turns up.

EXAMPLE

The following chart shows the OEX index and its 14-day Williams'
%R. I drew "buy" arrows each time the %R formed a trough below 80 percent. You can see that in almost every case this occurred
one or two days before the prices bottomed.

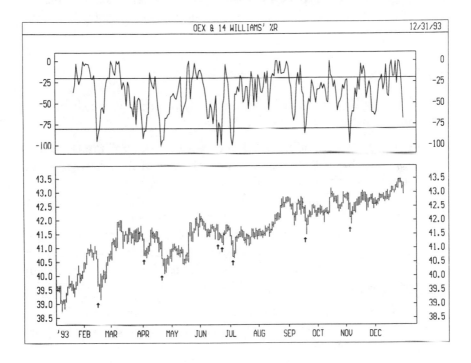

CALCULATION

The formula used to calculate Williams' %R is similar to the Stochastic Oscillator (see page 268):

$$\left(\frac{Highest\ High\ in\ n{-}periods\ -\ Today's\ Close}{Highest\ High\ in\ n{-}periods\ -\ Lowest\ Low\ in\ n{-}periods} \right) * -100$$

Zig zag

Overview

The Zig Zag indicator filters out changes in an underlying plot (e.g., a security's price or another indicator) that are less than a specified amount. The Zig Zag indicator shows only significant changes.

Interpretation

The Zig Zag indicator is used primarily to help you see changes by punctuating the most significant reversals.

It is very important to understand that the last "leg" displayed in a Zig Zag chart can change based on changes in the underlying plot (e.g., prices). This is the only indicator in this book where a change in the security's price can change a previous value of the indicator. Since the Zig Zag indicator can adjust its values based on subsequent changes in the underlying plot, it has perfect hindsight into what prices have done. Please don't try to create a trading system based on the Zig Zag indicator—its hindsight is much better than its foresight!

In addition to identifying significant prices reversals, the Zig Zag indicator is also useful when doing Elliott Wave counts (see page 125).

For additional information on the Zig Zag indicator, refer to *Filtered Waves* by Arthur Merrill.

Example

The following chart shows the 8 percent Zig Zag indicator plotted on top of Mattel's bar chart. This Zig Zag indicator ignores changes in prices that are less than 8 percent.

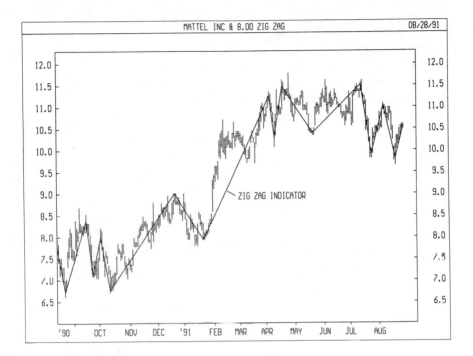

ZIG ZAG INDICATOR

CALCULATION

The Zig Zag indicator is calculated by placing imaginary points on the chart when prices reverse by at least the specified amount. Straight lines are then drawn to connect these imaginary points.

BIBLIOGRAPHY

Appel, Gerald and Hitschler, Fred. *Stock Market Trading Systems*. Homewood, IL: Dow Jones-Irwin, 1980.

Appel, Gerald. *The Moving Average Convergence-Divergence Method*. Great Neck, NY: Signalert, 1979.

Arms, Richard W., Jr. *The Arms Index (TRIN)*. Homewood, IL: Dow Jones-Irwin, 1989.

Arms, Richard W., Jr. *Volume Cycles in the Stock Market*. Salt Lake City, UT: EQUIS International, Inc., 1994.

Cohen, A.W. *How to Use the Three-Point Reversal Method of Point & Figure Stock Market Trading*. Larchmont, NY: Chartcraft, 1984.

Dobson, Edward D. *Understanding Fibonacci Numbers*. Greenville, SC: Traders Press, 1984.

Edwards, Roberts D. and Magee, John. *Technical Analysis of Stock Trends*. Sixth Edition. Boston, MA: John Magee, Inc., 1992. (Distributed by New York Institute of Finance.)

Fosback, Norman G. *Stock Market Logic*. Chicago, IL: Dearborn Financial Publishing, Inc., 1992.

Frost, A.J. and Prechter, Robert. *Elliott Wave Principle*. Gainesville, GA: New Classics Library, Inc., 1985.

Granville, Joseph E. *New Strategy of Daily Stock Market Timing for Maximum Profits*. Englewood Cliffs, NJ: Prentice-Hall, 1976.

McClellan, Sherman and Marian. *Patterns for Profit: The McClellan Oscillator and Summation Index*. Wayne, PA: Foundation for the Study of Cycles, 1989.

Merrill, Arthur. *Filtered Waves—Basic Theory*. Chappaqua, NY: The Analysis Press, 1977. (Available from Technical Trends, P.O. Box 792, Wilton, CT 06897)

Natenberg, Sheldon. *Option Volatility and Pricing Strategies*, revised edition. Chicago, IL: Probus Publishing Company, 1994.

Nison, Steve. *Beyond Candlesticks*. New York, NY: John Wiley & Sons, 1994.

Nison, Steve. *Japanese Candlestick Charting Techniques*. New York, NY: New York Institute of Finance, 1991.

O'Neil, William J. *How to Make Money in Stocks*. Second Edition. New York, NY: McGraw-Hill, Inc., 1995.

Pring, Martin J. *Technical Analysis Explained*. Third Edition. New York, NY: McGraw-Hill, Inc., 1991.

Wilder, J. Welles. *New Concepts in Technical Trading Systems*. Greensboro, NC: Trend Research, 1978.

Zweig, Martin. *Winning on Wall Street*. New York, NY: Warner Books, 1986.

INDEX

- X -

Xerox Corporation, 65, 308-9

- Z -

Zero-based volume, 9-10
Zig Zag indicator, 140, 318-19
Zweig, Martin, 75, 77, 139, 248, 296

ABOUT THE AUTHOR

Steven B. Achelis (pronounced "ə•kāy´•lĭss") is the founder, owner, and president of EQUIS International, Inc. His company is a leading provider of investment analysis, portfolio management, and stock market data collection software.

An experienced investment analyst and trader, Steve has published a number of articles on stock market timing and is the author of *The Market Indicator Interpretation Guide.*

He is also a gifted computer programmer and the author of a large number of programs, including the best-selling MetaStock software program.

Steve has appeared on various national radio and television shows including CBS and the former Financial News Network (now CNBC). When he is not immersed in investing and technology, he likes to spend his time windsurfing, snowboarding, and being with his family.